KU-114-773

THE

MUSIC LOVERS' PORTFOLIO

EDITED BY

LANDON RONALD

LONDON

Y BOOK COMPANY, LTD

INGDON STREET, E.C.4

with GEORGE NEWNES, LTD

CONTENTS.

LITERARY SUPPLEMENT.

THE

MUSIC LOVERS' PORTFOLIO

FOREWORD BY THE EDITOR

THE chief aim and object of myself and of all those connected with this new publication has been to provide Music and Articles about Music which will appeal to any and everybody who cares for the Art.

The items have been chosen with care and without prejudice for or against any particular school of music. The man to whom a Beethoven Symphony is anathema may find solace in some simpler and more tuneful Pianoforte piece. The lady who scorns the simple ballad that touches the heart may revel in the abstruseness of Brahms or the romance of Schumann.

Personally, I hope the idea of reducing the score of the gargantuan Fifth Symphony by Beethoven to an ordinary Pianoforte solo will appeal to the thousands of amateurs who know and love the work, but have hitherto had but little opportunity of playing it in their own homes. My colleague, Mr. Ernest Austin, and myself have endeavoured to keep to the original text as far as possible. It is our belief and hope that playing it in the family circle may help to recall many brilliant performances of the familiar work heard in our concert rooms under celebrated conductors.

Much care and thought have been expended on the choice of subjects which should make the reading section interesting to all. I have in every case insisted that they should be not so much for the musician as for the ordinary man in the street who loves music but does not want to be worried with the technical side of it.

Photo: J. Russell & Sons.

MR. LANDON RONALD

Everybody who has followed musical matters will readily admit that the best known critic and writer on the subject is Mr. Ernest Newman; and I consider it very fortunate that we are enabled to publish in this Portfolio many articles of exceptional interest from his pen.

There is an old and a true saying that "Good wine needs no bush." The worth of this Portfolio should speak for itself. We have given of our best and now it rests with the public to approve or disapprove of our efforts. I am prepared to stand or fall by their verdict, having confidence in their judgment and a belief in their acumen to take advantage of a good thing when they see it.

In conclusion, I may say that it is my wish that this Portfolio may help many members of the great public to a better understanding and appreciation of the Art I have the honour to serve. If it succeeds in doing this, the aspirations of its publishers and myself will be realised.

Landon Ronald.

HOW TO PLAY RACHMANINOFF'S "PRELUDE IN C SHARP MINOR"

by MARK HAMBOURG

THIS Prelude, in spite of being tremendously hackneyed, still remains one of the most monumental pieces of music for the pianoforte of its kind in existence, and its popularity shows no sign of abatement. The reason is not far to seek. In the first place it obviously possesses a significance which it is the task of the performer to interpret; and, in the second place, it is the work of a composer who is also a fine pianist, and knows how to write for his instrument. In other words, it is pianistic.

Sergei Vassilievich Rachmaninoff is a romantic personality, and certainly an outstanding figure in music to-day. Though he cannot be classed amongst the extremists, he is, nevertheless, truly modern in that his style shows a natural development of his particular gifts of melody and sonority, and that his later compositions prove him to be getting more profound and more polyphonic, besides making the most exacting demands as regards technique. As he is still in the prime of life, having been born at Novgorod on April 1, 1873, the world may reasonably look for more fine compositions from him. His musical talent was evinced at an early age, for he was only nine when he became a student of the pianoforte at Petrograd Conservatoire. After three years there, he proceeded to Moscow, where he studied for seven years at the Conservatoire with Zvierev and Siloti for pianoforte, and with Taneiev and Arensky for theory and composition.

Photo: Claude Harris.

MR. MARK HAMBOURG

His first appearance in England was at a Philharmonic Concert in 1899, when he conducted a performance of his "Fantasie in E," Op. 7, for orchestra, and also played two pianoforte solos—an "Elegy" and the "Prelude in C sharp minor." Although not a voluminous composer, Rachmaninoff has, nevertheless, produced a considerable quantity of works in almost every branch of the art—orchestral music, chamber music, songs and choruses, sacred music, operas, and, of course, music for his own instrument, the pianoforte, of which I would specially mention his three concertos, his preludes, and his very attractive variations on the theme of Chopin's "Prelude in C minor." During the last few years he has suffered, in common with many other artists, from the disturbed state of Russian politics, and has had to leave his native country. He is at present in America, where he is enjoying enormous popularity, both as a composer and as a pianist.

So much for the man. Now for the piece with which his name is indissolubly connected. It made his reputation with the general public, who imagined that the composer had worked to a programme. Regarding the nature of this there were all kinds of fantastic surmises put forth. If I repeat one of the least grotesque of these, it is not because I vouch for or even believe in its truth, but because it may possibly aid the student to gain some insight into the character of the music. Briefly, the story is to the effect that the music depicted the dejection of the exiles as they set out for Siberia with the clash of the bells ringing in their ears—a dejection deepening into despair, until finally hope reasserted itself, and the bells brought them an assurance of the ultimate triumph of right over wrong. Whether this be so or not, the effect of bells is obvious, while the immanence of deep feeling—nay, of acute suffering—is undeniable.

In placing before the reader my ideas of how this fine piece ought to be rendered, I should like to say that the interpretation now set forth is the outcome of my own personal feeling and of having performed the "Prelude" many, many times in public. It will be seen that I do not slavishly adhere to the printed expression marks.

For convenience of reference, it will be well to note the form of the piece, which is plainly divisible into three parts. The first consists of fourteen bars, the middle section (*agitato*) of twenty-eight bars, and the third part, which is an amplified version of the first, of thirteen bars, the last six bars constituting the coda.

The fundamental idea of the first part is that of two simultaneous themes. First, there is the motive of the bells in bars one and two, repeated and developed in succeeding bars; and then there is the melody above it, which is harmonised in chords. One sometimes hears the octaves played as if they, and they alone, were the melody, the chords being treated merely as accompanimental, a reading which robs the piece of its poetry and poignancy of feeling.

In starting the "Prelude" do not rush the *tempo* (incline rather to the slow side than the reverse); use the pedal very discreetly so as not to blur the effect, and do not indulge overmuch in *rubato.* The first two bars, which contain the key to the whole of the first section, must be brought out with great vehemence, the C sharp in particular being played with impressive force, and slightly prolonged beyond its written value. It will thus persist, while the upper melody enters gently, but still so as to be heard distinctly. The quaver figure in bars three, four, five, and six must be played, not with equal force, but so as to suggest a sigh, with a *crescendo* from the first chord to the second, followed by a *diminuendo.* This melody should, as it were, float above the bell motive, which is played forcibly throughout, the end of the passage having a *crescendo* to the pedal point G sharp in bar seven, which should be played *fortissimo.* Here for two bars we have a loud clangour of bells. Render bar seven with a slight *accelerando,* and bar eight with a corresponding *ritardando.* In bar nine the *pianissimo* returns, and the music is played as at first, but with a marked *rallentando* in bars thirteen and fourteen. Take care in bar eleven that the C sharp is held for its full value, and that in bar fourteen the quavers in the left hand are brought into prominence.

We now come to the middle section, *agitato,* and here note that I am re-numbering the bars as from this point. Do not begin it too quickly, as otherwise the effect of a later climax will be missed; and play it with a kind of muffled tone. The C sharp in the bass of bars one, two, four, and six should be struck rather sharply, with a suggestion of the clash of cymbals, the crotchets in the left hand in bars three, four, seven, and eight imitating the sonority of the violoncello. At the ninth bar the F sharp in the melody should be played with an accent, and an *accelerando* begun, coupled with a *crescendo* to bar fourteen, where there should be great sonority, the whole force of the piano being displayed, with but slight variation, and with ever-increasing speed, up to bar twenty-two. At the second half of this bar begins a passage which seems to suggest the culmination of absolute despair. This passage should begin with a slight holding back of the *tempo* for about four beats, after which it proceeds with ever-increasing impetuosity and tremendous tone as far as bar twenty-seven, where there is a slight *ritardando.*

After bar twenty-nine comes the return to the music of the original subject, first section, but amplified, the general volume of sound being much augmented. The bell motive, A, G sharp, C sharp, should receive great significance, bars one and two (re-numbering again) being exceedingly slow. It will be noticed that the composer has altered his marking of the emphasis to be given to the chords from bar three onwards; it is no longer the sighs, but a song of triumph, that we hear. Therefore the chords must be played strongly, though the chief accent still falls on the second of each group of three quavers. Bars seven and eight suggest the joy-ringing of bells in a great cathedral, and the *tempo* must be slightly, not markedly, quicker.

We are now coming to the end of this fascinating piece. After the exhilaration of triumph follows reaction. The effect of sighing returns (bar eleven) and for two bars there must be a *rallentando molto.* The *tempo primo* is resumed at bar thirteen, and there follows a *crescendo* from *mf* up to bar sixteen, which should be given triple *forte.* To secure an effective and appropriate close needs a little care. There should be in bar seventeen a distinct *ritardando,* the chord of the diminished seventh on the pedal point being given *diminuendo.* The last two bars should be as soft as possible, and the piece ends as if asking a question: "What, after all, does the future hold?"

So far as is feasible in print, the above represents my own interpretation of the "Prelude in C sharp minor," but, in conclusion, I cannot too strongly remind the student that a reading, to be really satisfactory, must be the outcome of the player's own artistic feeling and insight. Still, I am not without hope that these few suggestions may help him to a more intimate acquaintance with the significance of the "Prelude."

BEETHOVEN'S FIFTH SYMPHONY

by ERNEST NEWMAN

First and Second Movements

THE C minor Symphony of Beethoven is perhaps the most famous of the world's greater musical works. It has a sure hold upon the plain music-lover; and, in spite of all changes of style and of taste, it still commands the whole-hearted admiration of the instructed musician. It is a work that, so far as we can see, will never grow old—one of those works in which a composer puts forth an almost convulsive effort of the imagination, that endures like some inexhaustible force of nature. "Tristan" is such a work among operas. No music ages so rapidly as love-music; as we play the love songs of only two or three hundred years ago, indeed, we find it a little hard to believe that the men who wrote them and sang them were full-blooded creatures who put the whole passion of their souls into these songs. To us they seem pale, shadowy, touched not with passion but with a wistful melancholy. The love-songs of Schumann and Brahms, beautiful as they are, already seem like voices crying their lovely message to us across a gulf; we know that the men and women bodied forth in them were creatures like ourselves, yet there is something in them that marks them as being of a different civilisation from ours. But "Tristan" does not carry its date written upon it like this; it has all the nervous energy of our own nervous epoch. So with the C minor Symphony. It was born of some stupendous turmoil in the always suffering soul of Beethoven; and so vital is the expression of this turmoil that it lives again, after the lapse of more than a hundred years, in the soul of everyone who hears the music.

The symphony seems to have been begun in 1805 (when Beethoven was thirty-five), laid aside during the following year, and completed during 1807 or in the early part of 1808. It was first performed in Vienna in December of the latter year. It was something new in the history of music. The classical symphony, as the reader no doubt knows, grew up partly out of the older Suite (a string of dance movements), partly out of the song form. It had settled under Mozart and Haydn into a standardised structure. Roughly speaking, the form is one of four movements. The first is a weighty one in fast time, and is naturally followed by a slow movement, in which the composer draws upon a deeper well of feeling. The finale, again in fast time, prevents the hearer being left at the end with emotions that might sadden him. Between the slow movement and the finale the instinct of composers led them to interpose a short, slight movement—generally a minuet. This made the transition from the emotional, thoughtful second movement to the lively fourth movement less abrupt than it would otherwise be.

Every symphony, of course, was not constructed precisely on these lines, but this was the basic design. The first movement had a special and rather elaborate design of its own—a design known specifically as "sonata form." The basis of the design was the contrast and interplay of two "subjects." In the first, or "exposition" section of the movement, these two subjects were set forth and discussed both separately and in conjunction. In the second, or "development" section, they were shown in new metamorphoses, perhaps with the admixture of some "episodes" not thematically akin to themselves. In the final, or "recapitulation" section, a return was made to the subjects in their original form, and the music, after all its wanderings through near or distant keys, settled down again in triumph in the key of the opening.

Rischgitz Collection.

BEETHOVEN

At the time of this painting (1817) *Beethoven was in his forty-seventh year, and began the composition of the Ninth Symphony, which he finished six years later.*

In the earlier stages of the symphony there was no connection either of theme or of mood between the various movements, and the joinings of the three sections of the first movement were often very obvious. The instinct of the great artist is always to conceal his art. A scaffolding is necessary when a building is being put up; but the final object of the architect is to leave no trace, no hint, of the material means by which his result has been obtained. Beethoven had, in an extraordinary degree, the sense of *logic* in music. His artistic instinct told him that the first movement should not be built up in three separate blocks, as it were, but that one bar should run so logically, so inevitably into the next that the music should seem one organic body of thought from the first bar to the last. He felt also that a symphony that gave the impression that all the movements had something to do with each other would be better than one in which the movements seemed put together at haphazard. For a hundred years after him composers have been trying various ways of making a long symphonic work one organic whole. Beethoven's mighty effort to do this in the C minor Symphony was something without precedent.

How he does it will become more apparent when we come to discuss the third and fourth movements of the symphony. Here it will be enough to say that he first of all creates a logical connection of mood between all four movements and then emphasises the connection formally by using again, in the third movement, the most significant theme of the first. The first movement, put what interpretation we like upon it, is obviously a battle between the forces represented by the two chief themes. Of the pregnant opening subject Beethoven is reported to have said: "Thus Fate knocks at the door." We need not interpret this too literally; but we can be sure that this subject represents something harsh, imperious—fateful, if we will—that the second subject (beginning at bar 63) represents something gentler, more appealing, more consoling, and that the marvellous movement is a debate and a conflict between the two. In the slow movement the soul in which this mighty conflict has taken place rests for a moment and broods upon the beauty, the splendour, the pathos of life. The third movement shows the undermining of this mood by doubts and terrors; all the sinister forces of the universe seem to conspire to drag the soul down and drown it in horror and despair. At last the soul wrenches itself free, and, in the tremendous finale, steps out into the sunlight again, singing a full-throated, full-chested song of the joy of deliverance. It will be noticed that there is no break between the third and the fourth movements: the working out of the drama will not permit of the usual severance of them. It will be noticed, too, that at one point in the third movement there recurs a reminiscence of the sinister "Fate" theme of the opening movement. The whole symphony is thus the realisation of one great idea. To make a symphony that, to make it not merely a play of beautiful sounds and patterns, but the evolution of a drama, was a quite new thing. Equally new was the carrying over of a significant theme from one movement to another—as if a character who had been long absent from the stage suddenly stepped upon it again and dominated it—and the steady working out of the one poetic purpose from the first bar of the third movement to the last bar of the finale.

THE

MUSIC LOVERS' PORTFOLIO

THE ART OF THE SINGER

by CARRIE TUBB

THE voice, considered as a musical instrument, differs from all others, inasmuch as it is the only one not made by man, and, consequently, its quality, range, and expressive power vary according to the individual. It is this fact which compels the vocal teacher, in far greater degree than the teacher of any man-made instrument, to adapt his methods with the utmost readiness and resourcefulness to the innate capacity and natural gifts of each of his pupils. At the same time, there are, in each case, certain broad principles which form the foundation of singing as an art, and it is in the spirit of those principles that these few ideas are presented.

A fine voice is the gift of God, and, as such, is a precious possession which is to be prized and cultivated; but I would not have my readers think that it is the only desideratum, nor, perhaps, even the chief of the many qualities which go to the making of a good singer. There must be musical sensibility, a good ear, the power of expressing oneself in the words as well as in the music, personality, charm of manner, plenty of courage, perseverance, brains, concentration of mind upon the object to be attained, and last, and most necessary of all, a capacity for hard work. This seems a truly formidable list of attributes for one person to possess, and yet I dare say that not one of them should be lacking if success of a high order is aimed at. It is no easy matter to be a good singer any more than it is to be a good pianist or violinist, and it is useless entering for the prize unless you can stay the distance.

As the breath is the motive power of the voice, its management and control should receive the student's first attention, breathing exercises being practised every morning as a natural course in order to keep fit. I emphasise the words "every morning," because it is not possible when physically tired to secure that deep breathing which is so essential, filling the lungs with an ample supply of air; and because without frequent and regular practice it will not become so automatic as not to be thought about when singing. The aim should be to inhale slowly and to expand the lower part of the lungs, avoiding that quick intake which only inflates the upper part and is associated with the raising of the shoulders. The act of breathing should be neither seen nor heard.

Photo: Compton Collier

MISS CARRIE TUBB

The voice, of course, is generated by the vocal cords, but its correct placing is a matter of vital concern. If there is to be good tone and carrying power, the column of vibrating air must be directed as forward as possible, against the hard palate, so that the voice is in the mask of the face—which receives the pressure of the vocal cords—and not in the throat. By so doing, and by keeping the muscles perfectly loose, the stream of air upon which the voice depends is unimpeded. There must be no stiffness; directly the attempt to produce tone involves effort it is better to discontinue for the time being and to take a rest. If the desired result does not come all at once, the student must not be discouraged, but keep on trying. With care and perseverance the rigidity will disappear in time. The main thing to aim at is a perfectly natural and effortless emission of the voice.

As it is possible to produce tone only upon vowel sounds, consonants being but distinguishing noises, exercises must be sung to them. The first, and most generally useful, is the broad, open "*Ah*," *but all the other vowels should be used later on*. Many of our singers get into difficulties with their own language just because their devotion to "*Ah*" causes them to neglect the other vowel sounds, of which there is a considerable number in every language, and especially in English. The practice of the different vowels calls for great exactness and purity, for unless intelligibility is attained the singer has mistaken his vocation. The voice should be "stretched" every day in order to keep it supple, and exercised throughout the vocal range on arpeggios of the common chord and of the dominant seventh, rising each time by a semitone. The arpeggios should be taken at the beginning of the practice and be followed by scales and other exercises for half-an-hour a day. This regular daily practice is the foundation of good singing ; no singer can get on without it.

If these exercises have been thoroughly assimilated, enunciation will follow as a matter of course, particular care being taken to keep the jaw firm, without lapsing into rigidity. The vowels, in all their varieties, having been mastered, the consonants will demand attention next. Though not by any means so difficult as the vowels, they will require care in pronouncing them clearly and with good forward attack. Something more is needed, however, than strict accuracy to vowels and consonants ; not only must every word be clearly brought out, but elocutionary emphasis must be given to the essential or significant words. Get into the spirit of the song by studying the words separately ; by so doing the voice instinctively takes on the appropriate colour. If they are sombre, it becomes dark ; if they are cheerful, it beomes light. It is only when the character of the words has been thoroughly grasped that they can be wedded to the music in that perfect unity of expression which goes to make up an ideal interpretation. And here I would like to utter a very emphatic protest against the all-too-common sin of pulling the music out of shape, due to the mistaken idea that to do so is expressive and evinces temperamental gifts in the singer. It is nothing of the sort. It is not expression, but only very bad musicianship. The composer, who is, let us remember, a musician, gives his music a certain shape, and he has a right to expect that the interpreter should respect his creation, the outcome of both feeling and technical ability. It is quite easy for the singer to get his effects without breaking, and, therefore, spoiling, the original outlines of the phrases. Without any restriction of needful elasticity, the rhythm should be instinctively appreciated by the performer, who *must* religiously preserve it.

It is the very natural and proper desire of every performer to reach his audience. Experience will teach him largely how to do this, but it is a grave error to strain after making an effect. Effort and the appearance of difficulty will only distress and repel, making the judicious grieve, even though some groundlings may be impressed by what they do not understand. I am quite sure that the singer who feels sincerely, and expresses naturally and easily, the sentiment of a song will succeed in interesting and touching an audience. The sincere artist can always carry his hearers along with him, and get them to feel as he feels.

It goes without saying that singers who desire to retain their voices unimpaired should lead simple, healthy lives, avoiding late hours as much as possible, securing plenty of sleep, plenty of exercise, and plenty of fresh air. They need not be ascetic ; anything may be enjoyed in moderation. Constitutions, like voices, vary with individuals, and each must judge for himself what things are expedient. It is really a matter of common sense, enjoying the things of this life that suit him and avoiding those that do not.

My last word is a counsel of patience. The voice is an instrument which is necessarily slow in development, for the simple reason that its possessor is absolutely dependent on physical fitness and well-being. Mortal flesh is subject to so many ills, especially in a climate like ours where one is so peculiarly liable to take cold, that vocal study is sometimes intermittent and progress is consequently hindered. Besides that, it is no easy matter to bring under control an organ which is invisible to its owner and which may possess certain idiosyncrasies of its own. All difficulties, however, will be vanquished by assiduity rightly directed. So, above everything, *work hard*, and do not allow yourself to be discouraged.

WHAT IS GOOD MUSIC ?

by ERNEST NEWMAN

IT is much easier to ask the question "What is Good Music ?" than to answer it. It is true that we need not worry greatly over a little fact that seems, at first sight, to make the question itself superfluous—the fact that, with music as with everything else, one man's meat is another man's poison. No two people could be found who would agree at every point as to whether any given fifty works, say, were good or bad ; each would have his likes and dislikes. But it is obvious, in the first place, that when a man "likes" a piece of music it is because he thinks it "good" ; whatever it may be for other people, it is "good" for him ; and in the second place, if A thinks a certain symphony bad, and B thinks it good, each bases his judgment, unconsciously, on the same premises. The symphony seems good to B because it seems to him to answer to *his* notions of what a good piece of music ought to be. The symphony seems bad to A because it does *not* answer to *his* notions of what a good piece of music ought to be. The standard, the criterion that is to say, is about the same in the case of each of the two men : the difference in the judgments comes from the fact that, owing to differences of mental and physical and moral and temperamental make-up (to say nothing of differences of training, of early associations, and so on), B responds emotionally to something in the music that leaves A untouched.

We may illustrate the point in this way : Everybody agrees that there are good men and bad men, and everybody would claim to know a good man when he met him. But the same man may seem good to me and bad to my neighbour. Why? Not because we have different standards of what constitutes a good man. We should both insist that the marks of a good man were honesty, truthfulness, generosity, fidelity, and so on. But the particular man my neighbour and I were discussing might seem to me to possess these virtues, while my neighbour could not perceive them in him. One of us, broadly speaking, must be right about the man, and the other wrong. One of us may know him better than the other, may have observed him more closely. The point is that, even if we disagree as to whether a particular man is good or bad, we both admit that in order to be good he must comply with certain requirements—requirements that are the same for both of us.

Differences of opinion, then, as to whether this symphony or that is good music or not, need not worry us. It is good if it possesses certain qualities. If one man sees those qualities in it and another does not, that can be generally accounted for in the ways I have already suggested. We are under no obligation, in considering a question of this kind, to prove to anyone that a work that he thinks bad is good. Heredity, experience, temperament, training, example, associates, and all the rest of it have made different beings of us, and it is as hopeless to expect us all to take the same view of Beethoven as to expect us all to take the same view of Gladstone or Napoleon. We cannot be sure that we ourselves are always right, though we can rarely be brought to admit that we were wrong. But each of us claims to judge music not *qua* mere Jones or Brown, but *qua* human being. None of us is an ideal human being. If there were such a person, *he* would always be right. How then would *he* judge of the goodness or badness of music?

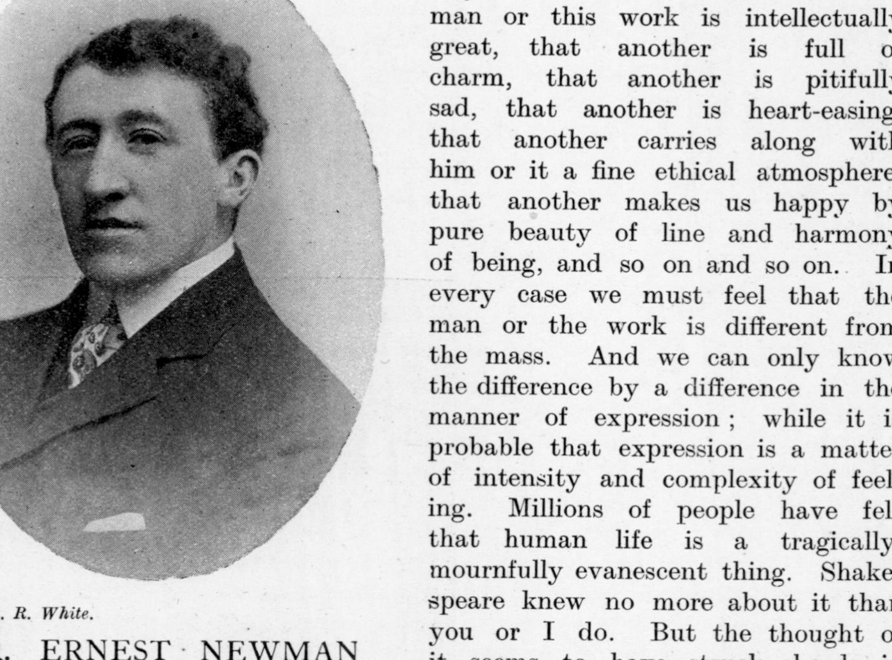

Photo: H. R. White.

MR. ERNEST NEWMAN

Well, he would first of all make short work of the bugbears of "form" and "technique," in the textbook sense of the terms. A musical work may be marvellously constructed, yet be of little or no account musically; while a work of the most rudimentary form and technique—such as a folk-tune—may be immortal. Nothing could be simpler in their make-up than a mazurka by Chopin or the little pieces that constitute Schumann's "Carnival"; but these give, and will always give, delight to musical souls everywhere, while many a symphony or an opera into which the composer has put ten thousand times the amount of thought and technique is as dead as a herring.

It may be supposed that sincerity in the composer is the test. But there is no reason for believing the writer of a good song, let us say, to have been more sincere than the writer of a bad one. The authors of the curious little poems that sometimes adorn the "In Memoriam" columns of the newspapers feel the deaths of their loved ones as deeply as Shelley felt the death of Keats; but they do not, for that reason, succeed in producing an "Adonais." Ethelbert Nevin, when he wrote the maudlin "Rosary," was no doubt as sincerely moved as Schubert when he wrote the "Ave Maria."

We could go on in this way, exhausting the list of things that good music is *not*; but that will not help us very much. We have to fall back, for something like a *positive* criterion, on personality. Some music is great and good just in the way that some people are great and good—in as many different ways, in fact. We feel that this man or this work is intellectually great, that another is full of charm, that another is pitifully sad, that another is heart-easing, that another carries along with him or it a fine ethical atmosphere, that another makes us happy by pure beauty of line and harmony of being, and so on and so on. In every case we must feel that the man or the work is different from the mass. And we can only know the difference by a difference in the manner of expression; while it is probable that expression is a matter of intensity and complexity of feeling. Millions of people have felt that human life is a tragically, mournfully evanescent thing. Shakespeare knew no more about it than you or I do. But the thought of it seems to have struck chords in Shakespeare that are not in our coarser instruments; and the result is the immortal

> "We are such stuff
> "As dreams are made on, and our little life
> "Is rounded with a sleep."

That great music, like great poetry, simply gives divine expression to the commonest thoughts and emotions of mankind, seems to be shown by the fact that the greatest music is the *commonest* music, in the sense that it is common to us all purely in virtue of our common humanity. It is significant that the very greatest works in each *genre* become the most universally popular, once they are really known. Perhaps, then, a rough working test of great music is this—that it bears endless repetition, that it becomes more significant the oftener it is heard, and that it appeals to every sort of mind, and to the musically untutored as well as to the expert. The great test, indeed, is repetition, as—to recur to our previous illustration—it is with people. We learn to assess people at their true value by living with them, or by seeing or hearing them every day.

The music that everybody, without distinction of age, of sex, of country, can bear to listen to any day and every day, is good music. There is hardly a musical comedy of ten or fifteen years ago the music of which would stand a revival; but the tunes of the "Beggar's Opera" are as delicious to-day as they were two hundred years ago.

WHY THE PUBLIC LOVES ORATORIO

by HERBERT BEDFORD

OF all the arts, the art of music is probably to-day the most progressive—or shall we say the most restless? New types of musical thought and musical expression succeed one another in number bountiful as the flowers of Spring. Some of them are nipped in the bud by an unkindly frost; but others, perhaps of slower growth, continue to flourish and send forth promising shoots.

But despite new musical methods, some introduced in all modesty, and some thrust forward with blatant advertisement—*the dogs bark—the caravan passes*—and the great public still goes to hear oratorio and loves it. And it is my purpose to inquire how this comes about.

Is it that the great public has convinced itself that Handel, Haydn and Mendelssohn are the supreme composers of all time? If so, has it arrived at such a conclusion by independent study—for the public reads little or no musical criticism?

HANDEL

Is it that the genus, Oratorio, can reasonably be considered to be the form of art that makes the most poignant appeal to the emotions or to the imagination? If so, what shape does this special appeal take, that has enabled it to capture the great heart of the people? Is it to be found in the structural grandeur of the Handel choruses; or in the sheer beauty of the melodic line that the master has given to the solo voices?

Is it in the courtier-like strains of Haydn, or is it in his brimming geniality—sometimes like a vision of Spring in the air, or again like a bewigged figure of "laughter holding both his sides"?

Is it the rhetorical, or, perhaps, the theatrical element in Mendelssohn that we must examine in order to find this special appeal that suffices to keep oratorio safe upon its throne?

It is assuredly not any one of these attributes, though it might conceivably be all of them. Indeed, they have the appearance of differing in their very essence, of differing so acutely as to contain no common factor. Yet common factor there must be, and, if it is not to be found in the music, we must seek it *in the audience*. And there we find it—and what is it?

It seems to me that this common factor is Familiarity—a familiarity dating from early youth—a familiarity with which is blended a fireside affection of old friendship; and the whole in an atmosphere of mental laziness, or, shall we say, of mellow inertia?

In common with the domestic animals, and the beasts of the field and the forest, mankind nurses a preference for the things that it is accustomed to. The new idea is suspect; and the longer the period through which we have been accustomed to any particular thing, or to any particular condition, the greater the suspicion with which we meet any innovation concerning it.

To the housedog an unknown visitor represents a new idea, and the pugnacious Towser barks or bites according to his temperament, or his temper.

The less energetic Snap investigates at a safe distance, but with suspicion in every bristle of his back.

The thoroughly lazy Fido possibly opens one eye; but there his interest languishes. He lets the unknown pass him by with never a murmur of inquiry, and returns to dream adventures among succulent bones.

In this great London of ours, a generation of musical folk that is now middle-aged, was spoon-fed in its youth with the Chamber music of the "Monday Pops." at St. James's Hall—a building long since demolished that we might eat and drink more and think less. A rather younger generation was musically reared on the Titanic strains of Richard Wagner. And so on, in succession down the years, until we arrive at groups of young people (bless them!) for whom music was born with the advent of the Russian ballet.

Each group is typical of a score of others, in that it is composed primarily of enthusiasts, of adventurers, ready to greet the unknown with a cheer. But who shall be found to hold that our great, solid, slow-moving public is consumed with the sacred fire of musical enthusiasm? Rather, would I say, is it permeated with what I have already called the fireside warmth of old friendship. And it is such mellow nectar that their parents gave them, and that they in turn give to their children, to the coming generation that, heedless of the adventurers and of the adventurers' enthusiasms, will still continue to find its pleasure in that music which, by sheer force of repetition through the years, it has come to understand, and to understand not as a critic, but as a lover.

Beyond all this, there is a comfortable feeling that in such music lies safety—with never the danger of shoals, with never the dread of a shock; and, knowing this music as they do, they found upon it a definite standard, equipped with which they can, in their more active moments, start out with confidence upon fascinating little excursions, either forward into the regions of criticism, or backward into the realms of reminiscence.

What, then, is the answer to our question: "Why does the public love oratorio?" Simply and solely this: That the public likes best what it knows best, and it knows this music best.

THE

MUSIC LOVERS' PORTFOLIO

HOW TO INTERPRET CHOPIN

by IRENE SCHARRER

NO one, in these days, would deny to Chopin a place among the great composers, or refuse him the homage due to a great master of unquestionable genius and originality. Yet, strange as it appears to us, it is on record that in the early part of his career he met with a lack of appreciation in some quarters. Thus a certain French critic found fault with the composer of the Impromptu in A flat, Op. 29, whose method, he said, was to hunt for an idea, writing and writing and modulating through all the twenty-four keys. If then the idea did not turn up—well, no matter! Do without it and finish the piece, *très bien.* This, of course, is absurd and unworthy of the name of criticism, but even so accomplished a musician as Moscheles, while acknowledging Chopin's charm and originality, asserted that his fingers, practise as he would, stuck and stumbled at his modulations, which he called "inartistic," "incomprehensible," "artificial," and "often forced." John Field also, a really gifted composer and pianist, sneered at his "sick-room talent." On the other hand, it is only fair to say that Chopin, when once he had got his chance in Paris, completely gained his public, and that brother composers like Mendelssohn and Schumann, paid tribute ungrudgingly to his gifts.

Photo: Claude Harris

MISS IRENE SCHARRER

Let us ask what are the outstanding characteristics of his music. First of all, I would emphasise the fact that it is perfect piano music; nothing before or since has been more absolutely pianistic, more thoroughly suited to the instrument. This was due, no doubt, to his being a pianist of rare and individual gifts, which had been trained and developed with remarkable skill by Elsner. In a letter to Elsner he asserted his resolution to create a new era in art. He was as good as his word!

Not only is it perfect piano music, but it also has a charm of melody and harmony which is peculiarly individual. Chopin is like no one else; and, though he has had his imitators, no one is quite like Chopin. His music possesses a romantic quality which is outstanding and gives depth and meaning to its charm. Another point that too often escapes the notice of the average performer is its flawless workmanship.

It is impossible to discuss the interpretation of Chopin's music without touching upon the question of *rubato.* To play it with metronomic accuracy is, of course, unthinkable, but, on the other hand, to be constantly breaking the time is an artistic offence. If we refer to Chopin's own practice we find that Moscheles said of it: "It is *ad libitum* playing, which, with the interpreters of his music, degenerates into disregard of time, but is with him only the most charming originality of execution." Liszt also described Chopin's *rubato* in these words: "Look at these trees! The wind plays in the leaves, stirs up life among them; the tree remains the same. That is Chopinesque *rubato.*" These utterances leave something to be desired on the point of definiteness, but one thing is clear — that Chopin's playing was never timeless, whatever the nature of the liberties he took. The idea of *rubato* in connection with his music has, however, become so firmly fixed with quite a number of people as to be a veritable obsession. What is the consequence? That in such inartistic hands Chopin's music becomes distorted, sentimentalised, emasculated. The *rubato* is used so frequently, and is so exaggerated as to obliterate the pure outline of the musical phrases. It should always be employed with the utmost discretion, so as not to break the rhythm. This is a point of supreme importance. If every trace of sentimentality were eliminated from performance, we should be better able to appreciate the true character of his music. The Barcarolle, the F minor Ballade, the Sonatas prove that he could write great music. These and others show a breadth of conception and a perfection of beauty equal to anything in the literature of music.

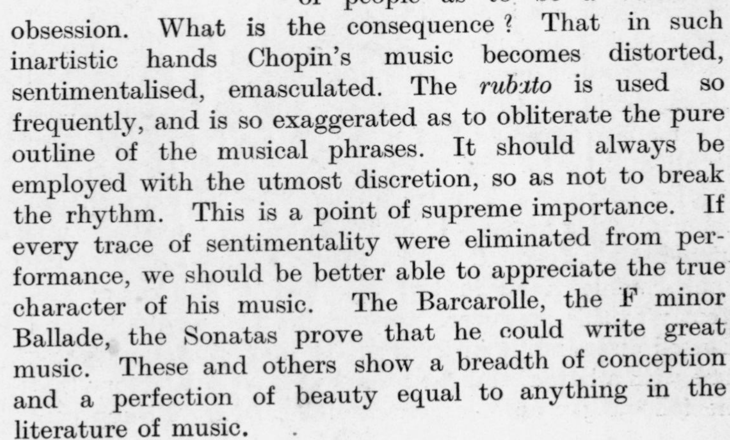

To interpret his works, therefore, is no easy matter. It calls for artistic restraint as well as great musical insight and expression. As in the case of all great music, one must live with it before being able to grasp it. Hopeless is it to try and interpret it without long and patient study.

It gives me pleasure to comply with a request to add a few words on how to play the popular Valse in D flat, known as the "One Minute Valse," which is given in this number of the PORTFOLIO, and with these I will conclude. In the first place, there should be no use of brilliant finger touch; I much prefer a warm, mellow tone, which is at the same time *pianissimo*. The chords in the left hand are often treated in a very unsatisfactory way; care should be devoted to playing their component notes with clearness and with an even balance of tone. The dotted minims in the bass of the second strain should be well, but not unduly, emphasised, so as to suggest a violoncello tone.

The middle section, which is marked *sostenuto*, may be taken a shade, but only a shade, slower. At the thirteenth bar of this part, play *pianissimo*, and four bars later (*dolcissimo*) use the *una corda* pedal. The long trill on A flat for four bars heralds the return of the original theme. In the last of the four bars (no left hand), which follow, introduce a slight *ritenuto*, which persists through the next bar; then there should be a gradual return to the *tempo primo* in the third bar of the theme. The last four bars I play softly, cutting out the *crescendo*, but retaining the *ritenuto* for the last two quavers of the descending scale, and finishing *a tempo* and *pianissimo*. The Valse otherwise is quite plain and straightforward.

CONDUCTORS AND CONDUCTING

by LANDON RONALD

IT is only within comparatively recent years that a good conductor has been recognised in this country as a great artist and worthy to be ranked among the most eminent of his profession. And even to-day there exist hundreds—nay, thousands—who are unable to differentiate between the mere time-beater, who wags a stick, and the *chef d'orchestre* who inspires all those under him to feel as he feels! But, fortunately, education is bringing us nearer to the better understanding of the Orchestral Conductor's Art, as is proved by the fact that recent concerts given in London by some of the most eminent *chefs d'orchestre* of the world have been usually financial as well as artistic successes.

Conducting, in the present sense of the word, was absolutely unknown in this country some sixty years ago—although some attempts had been made by Spohr, in 1820, at the Philharmonic Concert, to introduce a baton. This the Germans had been in the habit of using for a long time. The responsibility of keeping the band together was entrusted to the leader and a gentleman who presided at the pianoforte. The former would now and then beat time by tapping his desk with his bow, whilst the pianist would have a score in front of him and fill in chords when the band became refractory or uncertain how to proceed. The results can be better imagined than described, more especially when it is added that for each concert a different leader and a new pianist were engaged. We find among the former such names as Viotti, Mori, and Baillot, and among the latter, Clementi, Cramer, and Sir George Smart. The man to improve this uncertain state of things was Sir Michael Costa, who, after having trained the orchestra at Her Majesty's Theatre (under the management of Laporte) to a point of perfection never equalled, was offered, and accepted, the exclusive conductorship of the Philharmonic Band in the year 1846. Two years previously to this, however, Mendelssohn had visited us, and insisted on standing in front of the orchestra and beating time with a baton, and the results were so satisfactory that the following year Moscheles and Sir Henry Bishop continued the good work. But Costa was the one who insisted on the present-day concert system of conducting in this country, and since his time we have a long list of illustrious names of men who have followed in his footsteps.

It will always be hard for a musically-uneducated public to be able to distinguish between the three classes of conductors that thrive to-day, *i.e.*, the *artist* conductor, the *humbug* conductor, and the *bad* conductor; and it is proposed, therefore, to set forth here a few facts that may enable the ordinarily intelligent person to judge for her or himself. Thus, we will begin by mentioning the actual qualifications that an *artist* conductor must have:—

(1) He must be a thorough musician.

(2) He must have a good knowledge of the possibilities and distinguishing features of all the instruments.

(3) He must know the score of the work he conducts extremely well, and, if possible, by heart.

(4) He must have a good memory and an accurate ear.

(5) His beat must be clear and decisive, and indicate in an intelligible manner the different effects he wishes produced.

(6) He must be master of himself and of those under him.

Combined with these more or less mechanical qualifications must be such natural gifts as magnetism, soul, enthusiasm, and poetic feeling. How many of our greatest composers have possessed these latter qualities, but failed most utterly as conductors owing to their lacking some of the primary necessities named above! I will cite a few instances. Beethoven, that stupendous musician, was wanting entirely in that self-command and tranquillity that are so requisite. Even before deafness overtook him his useless gesticulations and ungovernable impetuosity confused and irritated his orchestra to such an extent that, in latter days, they would cease to regard

Photo : J. Russell & Sons.

MR. LANDON RONALD

his baton and proceed independently of him—keeping together as best they could. Schumann, who stands next to Beethoven in intensity of thought and feeling, was wholly lacking in the real talent for conducting, though he was director of some of the chief concerts throughout Germany. All those people, however, who can remember having seen him or played under him, declare him to have been unsympathetic, nervous, and, like Beethoven, wanting in collectedness and clearness in his meaning. That veritable Jupiter of Musical Art, Richard Wagner, succeeded Costa at the Philharmonic for one year, and gave the very greatest dissatisfaction ; and later on at the Albert Hall opinions differed so much as to his actual ability as a conductor that it is quite impossible to come to any definite conclusion. On the one side, we have the strongest testimony of his power ; and, on the other, equally convincing proof of his incapability. Since, however, there is "never smoke without a fire," we are inclined to believe that his marvellous knowledge of the orchestra, his wondrous poetic feeling and enthusiasm (as is shown in his works), and his own personal magnetism made everyone, except the hypercritical and the prejudiced, forget the other points that were wanting and which prevented him from ever becoming a great conductor

Thus we see that, as a rule, the greater the talent for composing the smaller the gift for conducting. But let us reverse the order of things, and see if great conductors have ever proved great composers. Looking down the list, we find that the gifts are rarely to be found in one man. Mendelssohn and Liszt stand out as exceptions to this rule. The former's power as a composer needs no comment, but as a conductor we are told he was exceptionally great. Liszt's compositions bear the stamp of true genius, and as a *chef d'orchestre* he was one of the most distinguished of his time. But Von Bülow, Costa, Facio, Richter, Levi, Nikisch, Mottl, Wood, and other equally illustrious names, have not given us any works that will live.

Photo : Claude Harris.

SIR HENRY WOOD

The immediate proof to an indiscriminate public that they are in the presence of the *humbug conductor* is, any outward show on his part; any gymnastic, dislocated, arm-twisted, body-worsted, head-shaken gestures! Jullien, the king of his kind, whilst conducting his own quadrilles, would go through all the pantomime of the subject they were supposed to represent, and, at the approach of the end he would suddenly seize an instrument near to him and play it, afterwards sinking back into a sumptuous velvet chair, apparently exhausted ! And yet for twenty years the name of Jullien was a household word ! Portraits of him still exist, showing his dress and bearing to have been as eccentric and anomalous as his conducting. Unfortunately, imitators of his school are as numerous to-day as they were thirty years ago—if not more so ; and what was hard to bear in the originator becomes despicable in his followers.

Photo : Elliott & Fry, Ltd.

MR. HAMILTON HARTY

The really *bad conductor* is the antithesis of his acrobatic *confrère*. He is listless, careless, indolent, indifferent, and appears as if he were constantly apologising for living. His orchestra pay no heed to his beat, and will be found to talk and laugh during the performance. He is in every way a harmful and dangerous person, and should be unmercifully annihilated and suppressed when and wherever he be found. Berlioz says of him : "Except in listening to great works already known and esteemed, intelligent hearers can hardly distinguish the true culprit, and allot to him his due share of blame . . . and the bad conductor—in presence of the public who would pitilessly hiss a *vocal accident* of a good singer —reigns, with all the calm of a bad conscience, in his baseness and inefficience."

I hope all those who read this short article will find it help them to discriminate between the good and the bad ; then it will have achieved its object. But it must be remembered that it is only possible to touch on the fringe of such a big subject in the little space that is at my disposal.

BEETHOVEN'S FIFTH SYMPHONY

by ERNEST NEWMAN

Third and Fourth Movements

IN the article on the first and second movements of the Fifth Symphony, I said that we must not take too literally Beethoven's remark, *à propos* of the opening theme, that: "Thus Fate knocks at the door." For one thing, we have no authority for the story but the rather feather-headed Schindler. Another legend is that the theme was suggested to the composer by the song of a yellow-hammer in the Prater. Still less credence need we give to the amiable Sir George Grove's theory that the symphony describes the love of Beethoven and Thérèse von Brunswick, the "Fate" theme representing "him," and the second subject "her." Great works of art cannot be explained in this sentimental fashion. It is not safe, perhaps, to "poetise" or "dramatise" the symphony on any but the broad lines suggested in the former article. No pinning of the music down to any particular sequence of literary ideas is necessary.

Apart from the tremendous forcefulness of the expression from moment to moment, everyone feels that the symphony is almost unique in the *oneness* of it all. Deep down in Beethoven's sub-consciousness there persisted the mood represented by that first theme—let us call it, for convenience sake, the "Fate" theme, since it is so generally known by that title. That wonderful theme is, in the purely musical sense, as truly a character as any in opera; it changes its moods, its expressions, its gait, its look, from moment to moment. In the first movement it is by turns stern, harsh, imperious, brutal. The whole symphony may be said to depend upon it, for we feel it to be there even when it is not itself sounding; other things in the music are what they are in virtue of their implied relation to this. That the theme had become a subconscious obsession with Beethoven is shown by the way it suddenly emerges into the foreground in the Scherzo, and again in the Finale.

The symphonic movement that is now known as the Scherzo grew out of the slightest of the (generally) four movements of the older symphony—the Minuet and Trio. Beethoven casts aside the minuet; the current of his thought is too mighty to be canalised within such trim and narrow banks. But like all the innovators whose innovations come to anything, he proceeds with a mixture of audacity and caution. He preserves the old mould, but he pours into it a new spirit. He links the Scherzo up psychologically with the first movement by basing a great deal of it on a theme that is obviously derived from the "Fate" motive (it begins in bar 20 of the Scherzo). The first and third sections of the Scherzo deal with this theme and its predecessor (bars one to nine), but in very different ways. Notice the harsh, domineering tone of the "Fate" theme as it is first given out by the horns (bar 20, etc.), and the power of it when the wood-wind take it up in a higher register; the scale of tone is still higher when it recurs in bars 31, etc., on page 66, and, again, for a moment or two, at the bottom of page 67.

If the reader will now turn to the final section of the Scherzo (where a return is made to the key of C minor, page 70), and trace the further evolutions of the theme, he will see that it is uniformly presented in much quieter tones. Everything now is veiled and mysterious; and the mystery culminates in the marvellous passage in staves 2, 3, etc., on page 72.

We will take up this point again in a moment. Meanwhile let us see what has happened in the middle section. This C major section (pages 68 to 70) corresponds to the traditional Trio. But what a Trio! Nothing in all Beethoven's music is so baffling as this. What kind of music *is* this, precisely? What is its mood? The most ardent Beethoven students read the most contradictory meanings into the Trio. Sir George Grove thinks it "extremely droll" at its first presentation, and "droller still" when it begins to make the famous "false starts" (page 69, staves five and six). Berlioz, in a famous passage, compares the theme (which is given to the 'cellos and basses) to the gambolling of elephants. It means, in truth, a different thing for each of us. My own feeling is that it is not meant to be humorous, though I cannot find any adjective that will characterise it as I see it. Humour and drollery are ascribed to it, I think, mainly because there always seems something comical in the great, clumsy double-basses playing rapidly. But Beethoven may well have been, on this as on other occasions, more or less oblivious of his instruments. He may have wanted the surge, the momentum of the basses, and not remembered the touch of the humorous there is about them. I feel the Trio as one of those colossal swinging melodies and rhythms that Beethoven hits upon every now and then, in which the very cosmos seems to have flung itself into a dance.

Let the reader note the art by which, at the top of page 70, this gigantic rhythm is made to melt imperceptibly into the main rhythm of the Scherzo, and how we are in a moment back again in the awesome underworld without quite knowing how we have been brought there. Next come those mysterious repetitions and metamorphoses of the main themes to which allusion has already been made, and then a wonderful passage—the hush of the strings almost into silence on a simple chord (top of page 72), through which we hear the drum mysteriously beating out the main "Fate" rhythm of the Scherzo. It is like some life-force stirring in the depths; this force pushes upward in a long crescendo, and we burst into the Finale with a sense of having come from deep underground into the light and the air.

The Finale need not be described in detail. Beethoven here employs bigger orchestral forces than had ever been used before in the symphony; trombones, double bassoon and piccolo are added. One jubilant theme seems to spring out of the throat of another; the movement of the music is like a torrent making its way to the sea; the reader will notice how cunningly a triplet motion is brought in every now and then to give a greater swirl to the flood. Just when the sense of gathering power seems to be coming to a climax, Beethoven breaks off curtly and re-introduces the "Fate" theme from the Scherzo, sobering and aweing us at once. But, like the stylist he is, he gives a magical new touch to the old material. One of the greatest strokes of genius in the whole work is the strange, haunting cry of the oboe that begins halfway through the last stave but one on page 90. The exit of the music from the stage is all the more impressive for this slight delay. The great C major theme of the opening of the Finale bursts out again; the other themes follow; the music gathers momentum by its own weight; and in the last page or two the speed of it is irresistible.

THE

MUSIC LOVERS' PORTFOLIO

THE BEST WAY TO STUDY THE PIANO

by I. J. PADEREWSKI

THE first quality for the piano student is a natural musical gift, and next for its cultivation the energy for hard work, and the important requirement of a good, thorough teacher.

The sane, healthy way to study the piano is to apply one's thought directly to the work, laid out methodically by the teacher, for a certain length of time every day. Four hours daily should be given to study; for an amateur, two hours is enough. In both cases the divisions of time devoted to practice should be not less than one hour.

Of course, in playing the piano, the fundamental factor is technique, but that word includes everything, not dexterity alone, but also touch, rhythmic precision, and pedalling. That combination is what I call technical equipment.

The length of time to be devoted daily to finger dexterity depends upon what stage of technical development the student is in. In any case one hour daily of this branch of technique is indispensable.

Photo: Donald McLeish
MR. I. J. PADEREWSKI

Begin your study each day with the five-finger exercises and the scales. Play them slowly, very *legato*, and with a deep touch, giving particular attention in the scales to the passing of the thumb under the hand and of the hand over the thumb. The real secret of playing rapid, brilliant scales is this quick, quiet passing of thumb and hand. The position of the hand is of great importance. In playing up the scale with the right hand, and in playing down the scale with the left, the part of the hand toward the thumb should be held considerably higher than the part toward the little finger. Thus, by raising the inner part of the hand next to the thumb, and dropping the outer part next to the little finger, there is more room for the thumb to pass under the fingers easily.

In descending with the right hand, and in ascending with the left, the position of the hand should be reversed—that is, hold the hand lower toward the little finger. You will then be partially prepared for the passing of the fingers over the thumb, and have also, as in the case of the first position mentioned, a shorter distance to go to strike the keys.

The positions of the hand are of utmost importance, not only in scales, but also in arpeggios, and passage-playing of all kinds.

People with thick fingers have a natural tone, and consequently little difficulty in developing a beautiful touch. Others will have to work a great deal before they acquire it. In the latter case the practising of slow passages with a deep touch, and without lifting the fingers very high, is most important. At the same time each separate tone should be listened to and its quality noted. The strong hand with the thick fingers may be held even, with the knuckles down, while the weak hand with long fingers should be held with the back ball-shaped or arched, with the knuckles up.

In the training of the hand a great fault is the bending out of the first joints of the fingers where their cushions touch the key. Such a position of the finger, its point bent out, makes a good tone impossible. Students should pay great attention to the "breaking down" of the last joints of the fingers; it is a difficulty that must be settled in the very beginning.

The ability of producing a *legato* may be acquired by careful fingering, and by the use of the pedal. In the first case the quick, careful passing of the thumb under the fingers is the practical factor, always studying slowly, with a deep touch, and listening closely to the binding together of the notes. In the second case the judicious use of the pedal is the aim.

It is a mistake to be afraid to use the pedal in playing scales. In quick scales the pedal may be most effectively used to give brilliance and colour, but only under a certain rule. Use it on the central portion of the scale, but never on the important or closing notes. This gives brilliance and colour to the quick, passing notes leading up to the climax; then, by shutting the pedal off, the final and important notes ring out with an added value, clear, firm, and effective.

Change the pedal with every change of harmony. In playing the lower notes on the keyboard its change should be still more frequent, because of the slow vibrations and the thickness of the tone in that part of the instrument.

The manner of holding the wrist should be individual, according to the need of the pupil, and must be decided by the teacher. Some play quick octaves and *staccato* passages by holding the wrist very high, while others employ a method exactly the opposite.

One of the most important things in piano-playing is relaxation, and absolute absence of stiffness or rigidity at the instrument. Before the study of technique, ease of attitude in the player must be fixed by the teacher. Poses and nervous movements cannot be too zealously guarded against.

Many think that they display a vast deal of feeling if they make frequent *ritardandi* and long pauses on single notes. I would call this over-sentimentalism simply the abuse of rhythm. Under this same head comes the exaggeration of the *rubato*, so deplorably frequent in the playing of Chopin. The only way to avoid this is to keep as strictly as possible to the rhythm and the *tempo*. Nothing is to be gained by such affectations but distortion of the composer's ideas.

As technical studies I recommend Czerny's Opus 740 and Clementi's "Gradus ad Parnassum," the Tausig edition. The Czerny is pure technique and the Clementi is extensive and brilliant. These, together with some special finger exercises by the teacher, suited to the pupil, will, for a considerable time, be quite sufficient in the way of purely technical studies. Afterward the "Wohltemperirte Clavier" by Bach should be taken up, and, in due course, the studies by Chopin.

It is only by playing the scales with strong accent, and the slower the better, that precision and independence of the fingers are acquired. First play the scale through, accenting the notes according to the natural rhythm. Then let the accent fall upon the weak note instead of upon the strong one, and play the scale, accenting every second note; afterwards place the accent upon every third note, then upon every fourth. This gives absolute command of the fingers. As regards some good compositions to study, of composers who, in general, would be of advantage to the student, and yet are neglected, I would first of all advise Mozart, because, with our modern nerves and excitement, it becomes difficult to play with calm and simplicity. And these are the qualities that are required by Mozart.

Mendelssohn's "Songs Without Words" are of admirable use in acquiring a singing quality of tone, and the style of writing for the piano is of the best. For brilliancy of technique, I would advise Weber.

For advanced pianists I would recommend Moszkowski among the modern composers. His compositions from the pianistic and pedagogic point of view are perfect.

ADELINA PATTI

by SIDNEY DARK

"THERE is only one Niagara and there is only one Patti."

These words were said by the famous Jenny Lind to Sir Arthur Sullivan after she had heard Adelina Patti sing at Covent Garden in the early eighties.

Adelina Patti was born in Madrid on the 10th February, 1843. She died at Brighton on September 27th, 1919. No man or woman has ever been quite so completely cosmopolitan. Her father was a Sicilian. Her mother was a Roman. She was born in Spain. When she was little more than a baby, her family crossed the Atlantic and she lived for years in America and made her first appearance as a singer in the United States. For many years her home was in Wales.

Patti's father and mother were both singers, and her mother, indeed, appeared in the opera of "Norma" a few hours before Adelina was born. The child herself began to sing almost as soon as she could toddle. In New York she was taken to the opera whenever her mother appeared, and when she was seven she could sing the most difficult arias. The famous conductor, Arditi, who heard her sing at this time, refers in his reminiscences to "the well-nigh perfect manner in which she delivered some of the most difficult and varied arias without the slightest effort or self-consciousness."

She received some training from her stepbrother, but nature had given her a super-beautiful voice, a remarkable ear, and a genius for the stage. She was little more than seven when she began to make public appearances as a singer in various cities in the United States. In November, 1859, when she was sixteen, she made her first appearance in opera at the New York Academy of Music in "Lucia di Lammermoor." During this first season she sang in no fewer than fourteen operas which, besides "Lucia," included Mozart's "Don Giovanni" and Verdi's "Traviata," "Il Trovatore," and "Rigoletto."

In May, 1861, Patti sang for the first time in London. The opera she chose was "Sonnambula." Her contract with Gye, who was then the manager of Covent Garden, was to give three trial performances for nothing. She was afterwards to be bound to Gye for five years, and to sing for a fee of a little over £30 a performance. London critics were not so enthusiastic as the New York critics had been. Faults were found with certain notes in Patti's middle register, and she was accused of occasional defects in style.

It would be tiresome to set out the long unbroken series of successes that followed the first European appearance of a young girl still under seventeen. Soon after her engagement at Covent Garden she was commanded to sing at a State concert at Buckingham Palace. In those days the programme at State concerts was confined to sacred music and Patti had to study Mendelssohn's "Elijah" and "St. Paul." Charles Dickens was among her early eulogists. In an article written in "All the Year Round," in December, 1861, the great novelist said:—

"She has a rare amount of brilliancy and flexibility. She has some 'notions' (as the Americans have it) of ornament and fancy which are her own, if they be not unimpeachable, say, the dry-as-dusts, in point of taste.

"If not beautiful, she is pleasing to see; if not a Pasta, a Malibran, or a Lind in action, she is possessed with her story. . . .

"For the moment the newest *Amina* has the ear of London. In the future Mlle. Patti may become worthy of having her name written in the golden book of great singers. Meanwhile, what a tale is here told, not merely of her great and welcome promise, not merely of her possessing that talent for success—charm—which is born into few persons and which cannot be bought or taught, but of the lasting truth and attraction of the music to which Bellini set the story of the innocent girl who walked across the mill-wheel in her sleep!"

It is interesting to remember that, although the child of Italian parents, Patti was more English than anything else, and that she learned to sing "Home Sweet Home," which was always her famous encore song, when she was a small child playing with her brothers and sisters in the streets of New York. She made her final appearance on the operatic stage at Covent Garden on July 4th, 1895, singing in "The Barber of Seville." Forty-two operas were in her répertoire, including, of course, all the hackneyed Rossini, Donnizetti and Bellini, but including also "Don Giovanni," "Aida," and Gounod's "Faust" and "Romeo and Juliet." The one failure in her operatic career was made in "Carmen," for which her voice was entirely unsuitable, "Carmen" really being a mezzo-soprano part.

Patti earned immense sums of money. In one eighteen months' tour in South and North America her fees exceeded a hundred thousand pounds, and in the latter part of her life she frequently received a thousand pounds for a single concert.

Photo: Dover Street Studios

MADAME PATTI

In July, 1868, she was married in the Roman Catholic church at Clapham Common, to the Marquis de Caux, equerry to Napoleon III. In 1885 she obtained a divorce in France from her first husband, and in the next year she married Nicolini, an Italian tenor, in Swansea. Madame Patti had already secured Craig-y-Nos Castle, which remained her home until the end of her life. Nicolini died at Pau in 1898, and in 1899 Patti, who was then fifty-six, married the Baron de Cederström, in the Roman Catholic church at Brecon.

In his book, "The Reign of Patti," Mr. Herman Klein says:—

"The exquisite purity of her style brought an added grace to the simple tunes of Mozart, a more delicate polish to the suave and rapturous melodies of Gounod, an almost classical dignity to the tragic periods and pastoral refrains of Meyerbeer. In a word, she touched no figure in the operatic gallery that she did not adorn. No wonder Verdi, when asked to name his three favourite *prime donne*, replied: 'First, Adelina; second, Adelina; third, Adelina!' In his estimation, with her *Leonora*, her *Violetta*, and *Aida*, she literally 'filled the bill.'"

The fame of singers like the fame of actors depends on the memory of their contemporaries. It is futile to attempt comparisons between the living and the dead. But as I have already said, no singer ever had such popularity as was the fortune of Adelina Patti, and few men or women have ever given their contemporaries such a mighty measure of pleasure.

HOW THE ORCHESTRA HAS DEVELOPED

by ERNEST NEWMAN

THE orchestra is to the composer what his colour-box is to the painter. We can imagine how hampered painters would have been had it been impossible for the manufacturers to supply them with certain primary colours, or with a wide range of shades of any colour; and we can see how every addition to the number of colours or shades will give a new impulse to the painter's imagination. So with the orchestra. Certain things simply could not be said and done in music until the necessary orchestral colours had been found; and with every increase in the number and the range of these colours comes an extension of the field of musical thought. That is true, needless to say, with regard to single instruments as well as with regard to the orchestra: had Chopin been born in the eighteenth century he would have been a very different Chopin from the one we know, because the tone and the scope of the old harpsichord were inadequate to express music of more than a certain degree of complexity and warmth.

However much the orchestra of to-day varies in numbers and in details in this place or that, its type is constant. It consists of four main divisions—strings, wood-wind, brass-wind, and percussion. This orchestra is the result of a long course of evolution. It will doubtless be modified in the future, but we can hardly imagine the *type* being greatly altered, just as the human type remains constant, no matter what physical or mental varieties it develops in different epochs and different countries.

The orchestra, in its present "type" form, utilises all the known methods of making musical sounds. These methods are three in number: (*a*) striking some resonant substance; (*b*) setting an air column in motion by blowing down a tube or across an opening in a tube; (*c*) setting a string vibrating by plucking it or by drawing some other substance, such as a bow, across it. Some instruments belong in part to more than one of these groups. Thus group (*a*) includes not only the recognised percussion instruments—drums, gongs, triangles, and so on—but the piano and the dulcimer, which are both percussion instruments and string instruments. Broadly speaking, however, these three types are distinct both in their modes of action and in the colour results they produce. The development of the orchestra has been the process of finding out the best instruments in each group, the best way to use them individually, and the best proportions in which to blend them. Each group has become of itself a sort of little community with laws of its own, and able to maintain a separate existence of its own. Music can be written for strings alone, or for wood-wind alone, or for brass alone: each group can supply a sufficient range of tone not only to make full harmonies but to get a fair amount of colour variety. Even the kettle-drums have been written for as a self-contained group.

At first composers were hampered in two ways: some of our modern instruments did not exist, or had not their present perfection; and of existing instruments the composer could use only those that happened to be available where he was working at the time. The orchestra used by Monteverde in his opera "Orfeo" (1608) was to our eyes a haphazard collection of most of the instruments of the day—harpsichords, harp, violins and viols, cornets, trombones, flute, clarion, trumpets, guitars, and a small organ. Evidently such an orchestra was both redundant and insufficient: certain things would be multiplied to excess by different instruments, while other things could not be expressed by any of them. And in the eighteenth century, even though an instrument existed, it might not happen to be just where a composer was at the moment, and so he could not use it. Bach's system of instrumentation in different works obviously depended on what his resources were at the moment. Mozart was a passionate admirer of the clarinet, for which he has written beautifully in a number of works. But there is no clarinet part in one of his latest and greatest symphonies—the "Jupiter"—the reason, no doubt, being that he could not count on a clarinettist in the Court orchestra for which he was then writing.

Gradually each group of the orchestra came to perfection—or, at any rate, to efficiency—composers began to learn the art of combining the groups and blending their colours, and the constitution of the orchestra settled down into what it now is. There have to be enough strings to balance the brass and wood-wind at their loudest. Owing to the greater natural force of wind tone in general—one oboe or one trumpet, for instance, will cut through an orchestral *forte* where a single violin would be inaudible—not so many wind instruments are required; but the modern tendency is to use more of them, so as to allow of their making pretty full harmonic masses of their own. An ordinary late eighteenth century symphonic orchestra would have one flute, two oboes, two bassoons, two horns, and two trumpets. Composers to-day like to have their wood-wind in threes, if they can get them. Four horns and three trumpets are the standard number, but some composers employ, on special occasions, six or eight horns and five or six trumpets. They would no doubt write more frequently for very large orchestras but for the matter of expense. It is the German composers generally who affect them, because, owing to the large number of good military bands in Germany, it is always easy to get a few competent extra brass players for a special performance; whereas in England they would have to be brought from a distance.

The string section of the orchestra needs no description. Every one knows that with its first and second violins, violas, violoncellos and double basses it covers a very wide range of tone. The wood-wind and the brass-wind have their own distinctive tone-colours; but the reader should note that these have nothing to do with their being made of brass or wood. The differences in colour—in timbre—come from the different ways of setting the air in them in vibration. In the flute, the tone is produced by direct blowing across a hole cut in the neck of the instrument. In the other wood-wind, the vibrating medium is the reed into which the player blows. The clarinet has a single reed, the oboe and bassoon have a double reed, shaped thus ( ). In the brass instruments, the reeds are the players' lips, operating on a cup-shaped mouthpiece in the trumpet, trombone and tuba, and a funnel-shaped mouthpiece in the horn. A shallow cup gives a brilliant tone, as in the trumpet; a deeper and broader cup the heavier brass tone. (The bugle mouthpiece is a mixture of cup and funnel). Two methods are used in the brass for altering the length of the air-column so as to get notes of different pitches—valves or pistons, as in the horns, trumpets, cornets, tubas and valve trombones, and slides, as in the slide trombone. For completeness' sake it may be added that wind-instrument tubes are of two sorts—cylindrical (clarinet, etc.) and conical (oboe, bassoon, etc.).

The staple orchestra consists of a variable number of strings, two flutes, piccolo, two oboes, two clarinets, two bassoons, four horns, three trumpets, three trombones, tuba, and kettle-drums. As has been said above, the wind are variable factors. Supplemental instruments are the harp, the cor anglais (an alto oboe), the bass clarinet, and the double [deeper] bassoon. Percussion is used according to the fancy of the composer or the nature of the music; it may include any or all of the various drums, the triangle, tambourine, cymbals, gong, bells, glockenspiel (steel plates hit with hammers and giving bell effects), castanets, xylophone (wooden bars struck with hammers), celesta (steel bars struck by a sort of pianoforte mechanism: the instrument looks like a tiny piano), the anvil, the wind-machine, the rattle, etc., etc.

There are several wind-instruments not in general orchestral use. The saxophone is made in seven sizes, not all of which are quite practicable. It is a beautiful instrument—a sort of cross between wood-wind and brass-wind, made of brass, with a conical tube, and played with a single reed, like the clarinet. The lovely bass flute is too rarely employed. The sarrusophones (brass, with double reed), made in six sizes, were intended by their inventor to be possible substitutes for the oboe and bassoon.

All these extra instruments have their individual colours, and composers would use them more frequently if they could be sure of the scarcity of players of them not standing in the way of performances.

At a recent concert in Paris the Italian Futurists produced a number of new musical, partly musical and non-musical instruments (bruiteurs—noise-makers), out of which, according to them, the music of the future is to be made. It may be a little time yet before these come into general use. It is not every one who, like Signor Russolo, the inventor of these instruments, has ears for the music of carriages bumping along the road, the plaints of cats and other animals, the gurgling of gas and water in pipes, the strident cries of steam saws, and so on. For a little while longer composers will probably stick to the orchestra of Wagner and Elgar.

THE MUSIC LOVERS' PORTFOLIO

CHOPIN, THE POET OF THE PIANO

by VLADIMIR DE PACHMANN

OF all composers, not one is so generally popular or so widely appreciated as Chopin. Yet it is safe to say that the works of no other composer are so horribly murdered by the amateur and the mediocre pianist. This is primarily because Chopin is played more than any other composer by the amateur and the mediocre pianist.

Musical insight is a possession of which few can boast in an active sense, although many possess it passively. With proper musical training it can be acquired to some extent, but real genius in this respect is God-given ; it is as a tiny speck of yeast, which grows and expands with the mind until the whole soul of the artist is leavened. The passive appreciation is a different matter. If one walks through an exquisite garden, full of rare and beautiful flowers, one cannot but admire and appreciate the work of the gardener. But what proportion of those walking through such a garden could as successfully perform the gardener's task ?

The beauties of music, when properly brought out, appeal just as spontaneously as the beauties of a garden. The uncultured mind appreciates them immediately and indiscriminately, the cultured mind appreciates them spontaneously and discriminately, yet the productive ability in both cases may be equally lacking. Thus it is that Chopin suffers at the hands of the thousands of pianists who attempt to play him, for, while they can appreciate his beauties when they are shown to them by others, they do not possess the ability to bring them out themselves. His works contain countless beauties, but these must be read not only upon the music but between the lines, for to properly interpret the poetry and emotionalism of the composer it is necessary to mentally create the same atmosphere as that in which he lived. For Chopin came into existence at a time of great political restlessness among his countrymen the Poles, and the surrounding influences of his time were reflected to an extraordinary extent in all his works.

Photo : Claude Harris Ltd.

VLADIMIR de PACHMANN

To make a beautiful thing ugly is a very easy matter indeed. But to make an ugly thing beautiful is the most difficult of tasks. Yet it is a task that even Chopin occasionally demands. It is not to be supposed that all the work of any great man could possibly be of the same high standard, and Chopin is no exception to the rule. About one-third of his compositions are comparatively poor, and are, in consequence, not played at concerts. Amateurs need only interpret those pieces specially fitted to their own temperament.

This leads me to a point which I would specially urge upon all who play the piano. Each should early discover which particular works appeal most readily to his or her temperament. These should then be carefully studied and mastered one by one. Each piece that is thoroughly understood will open up some new avenue of thought which will in turn make possible the interpretation of some fresh and more complicated work. No piece can be mastered very quickly. Often it is a matter of years before one fully appreciates all the meaning and beauty of a passage.

Chopin-playing requires, above all else, an education amongst the works of other composers, not only because familiarity with other composers educates the musical understanding and cultivates a variety of temperament, but for technical reasons. The compositions of other composers may in some cases be more uniformly difficult than Chopin technically, but the works of no other composer combine such a variety of technical difficulties in individual pieces. To play Chopin, therefore, one must have thoroughly mastered all the means that every composer makes use of to obtain effect. And on top of the variety of technique required comes the special study of the true Chopin *pianissimo*. Of so delicate a nature are some of Chopin's passages that to do them full justice, and to bring out all their beauties, careful and special study must be made of *pianissimo* effects. This can only be acquired by constant effort and practice, but it is absolutely indispensable for the renderings of the works of this master.

Another small technical point which the amateur must master is the ability to accentuate some particular note in a chord. It often happens that Chopin's melody—the melody that lends meaning to the whole piece—lies in the top notes in a series of chords. If all the notes of those chords are played with an equal accent the melody is lost and the whole meaning of the passage destroyed. The melody, therefore, must be accentuated and brought out, while the other notes of the chord must be heard like an accompaniment. Often the same passage of chords is repeated several times in a given piece. Such passages should never be rendered in exactly the same way each time. The difference may be simply a matter of tone, but an even more striking effect may be sometimes obtained by neglecting the original melody and accentuating the second note of the chords, which will thus sound like an alto echo to a treble voice. Such effects as these are arrived at by careful thought and study, but they often transform passages that would otherwise be comparatively uninteresting into bars of great beauty and attractiveness.

CHOPIN

The necessary technique for playing Chopin could never be acquired by reading anything that I or another might write, but it is possible to draw attention to noteworthy points in connection with specific pieces, and with this end in view I will run through a few of Chopin's works that are most familiar to amateurs.

The mazurkas I will dismiss in a few words. In them Chopin displays some of his most changeable moods. When playing them one seems to be dancing with, so to speak, the tears in one's eyes all the time, for there is often an underlying note of sadness throughout the theme. Occasionally they break off into utter gaiety and wild, inconsequent joy. Sadness and joy are, indeed, strangely mixed up in them.

The preludes are always popular both with players and with audiences. The first of them reminds one very forcibly of Schumann. To play it is very refreshing, like a draught of cool spring water on a hot day, but the second is, I think, somewhat poor. The third, though it has not a very high meaning, is a delightful little prelude. The melody is so smooth that it reminds me of oil floating upon water, while a sort of zither accompaniment is running. The fourth, though more poetical than the second, would have been more attractive if written in the shape of a song for a lady's voice accompanied by a little harmonium. The fifth is one that is so difficult to properly interpret that one of the great pianists of the day once stated that he studied it for years before he ventured to play it in public. No. 6 could very well be played by a 'cello and violin, but it is possible on the piano to get more effect than could be got with the 'cello itself. The seventh is gay, the eighth an exercise, the ninth makes me think of returning after a funeral, and in the tenth Chopin seems to me to imitate his master, Hummel.

No. 11 is a fine prelude. There is melody all the time, and at this point in the preludes we begin to get genuine Chopinism. But it should not be played *vivace*! It should be *allegro moderato*. Liszt thought this prelude was nonsense if played *vivace*. In the 12th Prelude, again, there is a mistake very commonly made as to the manner of its playing. If it is played *presto*, all the beautiful poetical meaning is lost, and it becomes a *tour de force* only. If it is played *poco presto*, however, not only does it remain a *tour de force*, but all the poetry in it can be brought out.

I do not like the 13th Prelude. The 14th is all fun from beginning to end—a regular volcano of gaiety! The 15th is my favourite. It reminds one of an impromptu. The 16th is my great favourite! It is *la plus grande tour de force* in Chopin. It is the most difficult of all the preludes technically, possibly excepting the 19th. In this case *presto* is not enough. It should be played *prestissimo*, or, better still, *vivacissimo*. No. 17 is very majestic, and in it Chopin introduces harmonies not previously found in other composers. The 18th is really a cadenza. In it Chopin never repeats himself. From beginning to end it is brilliant and interesting. No. 19 is another one I am very fond of, but I think it the most difficult thing in the world to play.

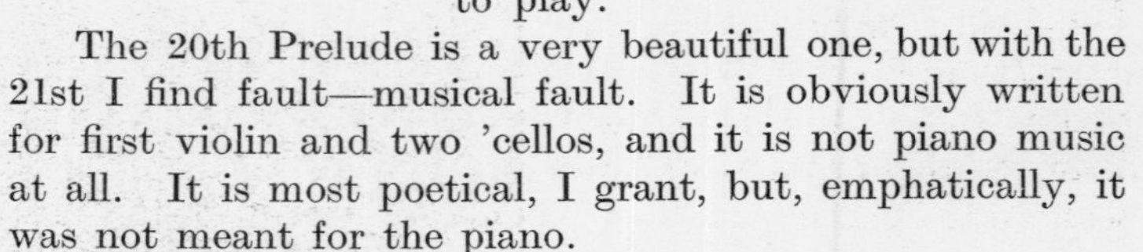

The 20th Prelude is a very beautiful one, but with the 21st I find fault—musical fault. It is obviously written for first violin and two 'cellos, and it is not piano music at all. It is most poetical, I grant, but, emphatically, it was not meant for the piano.

In the 22nd Prelude Chopin created energetic modern octave play. It was the first prelude of its kind in the world. In the 23rd Prelude pretty well all editions indicate short *legato* passages. Chopin never played such passages. He sometimes introduced a long *legato* passage, but never short ones of a few notes only. In the 24th the amateur would do well to remember that the whole beauty of this prelude is generally spoilt by the left-hand notes being banged. They should be *masqué* the whole time and should never be allowed to drown the right hand.

So much for the preludes. They are very beautiful and are worthy of the closest study and pains, not with a view of perfecting any stereotyped manner of playing each one, but of discovering the various methods which may be employed to bring out their beauty.

The amateur, almost without exception, practises them through and through in order to become technically perfect as regards the actual playing of the written notes. He or she thus produces an absolutely colourless study almost entirely without interest and quite devoid of meaning.

Perhaps more than any other composer Chopin requires deep thought and study, for his nature was such that he created, quite naturally, particular effects of tone and colour arrived at by none of his predecessors. These effects cannot be merely copied from the works of anyone else, so that Chopin-playing becomes a special study in itself, requiring special training and special methods of interpretation.

Even his most simple pieces are among the finest gems of our musical literature. Look at the études! Their worth does not lie in their merits from the point of view of musical construction, but in their immense poetical beauty. The very first one is among the harmonical wonders of the world. Yet this was written when he was but a youth of twenty!

Yet, with the études as with the preludes, each will be meaningless if improperly interpreted. Many of the most beautiful pieces of poetry in literature would seem uninteresting and flat if read by a bad reciter. In the same way, a good reciter will make attractive a poem whose beauties are not so apparent. A fine painter will light up each little beauty in his pictures until the smallest detail is attractive and strikes the eye. It is only the mediocrity whose work is characterised by sameness and lack of interest. There must be no mediocrity in the playing of Chopin.

HOW TO GET THE BEST OUT OF THE PIANO-PLAYER

by ERNEST NEWMAN

I.

THE answer to the question "How to get the best out of the piano-player?" obviously depends on what sort of "best" it is that you want to get out of it—whether you want to shine as a performer on the instrument, or whether you want to use it as a means to musical education. We had better consider both aspects of the question in turn.

Let no one think that because the piano-player, in a sense, plays itself, it is therefore easy to play well. Artistic results can be got from it, but only as you can get artistic results in anything else—by intelligent hard work. The fact that the instrument will play any notes that are cut for it does indeed absolve the performer from the necessity of acquiring a finger technique. But a performance in which the mere notes are played is as dull as a pianoforte performance of the mere notes would be. Pachmann's playing of a Chopin nocturne may be no more accurate, and technically no better, than that of the young lady next door; the difference between the two performances comes from something that is in the one and not in the other, an *expressiveness* that we cannot define, but that we know well when we meet with it. It is this expressiveness that you must add to the notes that the piano-player plays for you if you want to give an artistic performance.

A well-cut and well-marked roll will of itself do a great deal for you. The notes are right. If you follow the metrostyle line your general tempo will be right. The themodist* device will of itself bring out certain notes or phrases that need to come forward from moment to moment. But there is still a good deal left for the player to do. The rhythm of the music (not the same thing as mere accuracy of time) must be vitalised. The general movement of the music must be varied by all sorts of little hastenings and slackenings here and there; just as in speaking we do not preserve a uniform click-clack of tempo throughout, but vary the pace according to our feeling. Certain notes or melodic lines must be made to stand out, often in an inner or lower part. If the instrument does this already, to some extent, of itself, it must be assisted to do it better; if it is not doing it of itself, it must be made to do it. And just as, in speaking, we vary the loudness and softness of our tones and the force of our accents, so musical melodies should have all sorts of subtle little inflections in them, little variations both of loudness and of energy. A bad musician delivers a melody in one straight line, like a railway train running along a straight pair of rails; an artist delivers it in a series of swift little dips and darts, like the free flight of a bird.

To do all these things with the piano-player requires in the first place a technique, and in the second place artistic feeling and insight. In truth, the latter ought to be mentioned first, for with the feeling and insight there to begin with, half the technical battle is already won, whereas without them the piano-player performer will get no further than the hand pianist can without them. We will suppose, however, that you have been born with artistic feeling. The first thing to do, then, is to master the piano-player technique. You must practise till you know all that the instrument can do in the way of accenting and shading, and then practise still more till you can *make* it do its all whenever you like. And you must practise with method. You would never expect to learn to play the piano by skimming through half-a-dozen

* I use the terms "metrostyle" and "t emodist" to denote devices that are much the same in essence in different makes of instruments and of rolls, though the trade names for them may vary.

new works every day. You can only get a pianoforte technique by isolating each difficulty in turn and working away again and again at an exercise that embodies this particular difficulty—scales, thirds, sixths, octaves, arpeggios, and so on. You will have to work at your piano-player technique in the same systematic way.

Practise, first of all, to get complete control of time and rhythm. Pick out one favourite piece and stick to it for a while. Try the effect of all sorts of speeds, and of all sorts of little variations within each general speed. Get to feel the piano-player under your feet as a horseman feels his horse or the driver his engine—a living, sensitive thing that he can make responsive to a touch. Then practise picking out notes and phrases from the main tissue and making them stand out. Do it wherever you feel like it and think you *can* do it, whether the music really asks for it or not; at present you are playing not for the music's sake but for your own—to get a technique. Then practise the same phrase—some lovely thing that you are especially fond of—again and again in every sort of way you can think of, accenting it now sharply, now faintly, now holding it back, now urging it forward, making it now gently expressive, now hard as metal. Try to do with it all that a fencer can do with his sword.

Carry out these principles in every variety of detail that occurs to you, remembering that your object is that of any other aspirant after technique, to isolate one difficulty at a time and experiment with it till you have overcome it. Keep to one thing at a time—blowing, accenting, shading, pedalling, or whatever it may be. At first you will be woefully discouraged; the more carefully and thoughtfully you go about the business, the more difficulties you will light upon, and the more insuperable some of them will seem. But if you persevere you will find yourself overcoming them, and actually inventing new ones for the joy of overcoming them. Now and then, when playing a piece through, you will be astonished at some happy effect you have got without trying for it or thinking about it. Stop at once and take that passage again, and try to discover what it was you did that had such excellent results. If you cannot repeat the effect at once, as will probably happen, so much the better; it will make you think all the harder, and when you have tracked it to its secret cause you will have acquired a conscious technical mastery of it that will always be useful to you.

Finally, learn some little piece by heart that the great pianists are always playing—a Chopin study, for instance. The next time you hear one of them play it, note and memorise the little touches of style that gave the performance its beauty. Then go off home at once and try to reproduce them on your piano-player.

In a following article I shall try to show how to get the best out of the piano-player as an educational medium.

"THOU ART LIKE A FLOWER"

IT may seem paradoxical that the cynical German poet, Heine, should have written some of the tenderest love-lyrics in any language. But he did write them, and they are really beautiful lyrics in the genuine sense of the word.

"*Du bist wie eine Blume*" ("Thou art like a flower") ranks amongst the best. This delicate poem has tempted at least twenty-five composers, including some of the highest rank. The poem was written during Heine's holiday at Cuxhaven, on the shores of the Baltic, in 1823, and there is little doubt that its inspiration was mainly due to the fascination exercised over him by his beautiful cousin, Amalie, his first love. It first appeared in book-form in the "Reisebilder" (Travel Pictures), and afterwards appeared in the collection entitled "Die Heimkehr" (The Return). Among the great composers who set this lyric to music was Rubinstein, though best known as a great pianist—his last appearance on a concert platform in England was in 1887. His treatment of Heine's beautiful lyric is most apt, a simple melody suiting the simplicity of the words.

HEINE
the Author of the poem "Thou Art Like a Flower."

Liszt, another great pianist, whose appearance in England (1886) at the Royal Academy of Music shortly before his death is probably in the recollection of many people living, has produced a more organic setting. He skilfully uses the introductory figure both in the voice part and the accompaniment, most aptly conveying by that method the feeling of yearning which underlies Heine's words.

Schumann, as a composer, towers above Liszt and Rubinstein, as is shown in his version of this song. Nothing could be more inspired with tenderness than the melody he has written to the poet's delightful words, while the accompaniment, rich though simple in design, seems to be the ideal counterpart of the melody.

We print in this number the setting by Schumann, and in Part 10 we shall print the setting by Rubinstein, and in Part 15 that by Liszt, which will enable an interesting comparison to be made of the different ways in which this beautiful lyric has appealed to three great musicians.

WOODLAND SONG.

SOLO FOR THE PIANOFORTE.

G. H. CLUTSAM.

pp
f
3
3
p
cresc.
dim. e rit.
molto
a tempo
p
rit.
pp
meno mosso
rit.
pp rit. al fine

BLESS YOU!

Words by
DOUGLAS FURBER.

Music by
IVOR NOVELLO.

nev - er des-pair, Bless you for wait - ing, nev - er hes - i -
poco rall.
tempo
- ta - ting, Bless you, Bless you!
poco rall.
tempo
pp
pp
Some-times when the sha - dows are deep, Some-times when the
world is a-sleep Sor - rows fade a - way, Your voice seems to

say — Bless you for the trust that is there, Bless you, that you
nev - er des - pair, God will re - quite us, He will u -
- nite us, Bless you, Bless you for the
rall.
sun in your eyes, Bless you! —
ten.
ten.
p
pp
L. H.
ppp

PRÉLUDE.

S. RACHMANINOFF, Op. 3. № 2.

ppp
Agitato.
mf
cresc.
dim
mf

cresc
dim.
cresc.
ff
dim.

cresc.
fff
fff
ff
fff
ff

R. H.
fff pesante
sffff
L. H.
fff pesante
sffff
sffff
sffff

dim.
dim.
mf
dim.
ppp
mf
dim.
ppp

WINGS OF SONG.

Andante tranquillo.

Mendelssohn.

cre - - - - scen - - - - - - - - - do
fair, The lo - tus blos-soms are wait - - - ing To
cre - - - - - - scen - - - - - - - - - do
dim.
greet thee fond - ly there, The lo - tus blos-soms are
p
dim.
pp
cresc.
p
wait - - - - - ing To greet thee fond - ly there.
p
cresc.
The
f
dim.
p

vio - - lets there are all laugh - - - ing, And gaze at the sky far a -
p
bove, Se - cret-ly tell - ing the ros - - - es Sweet -
fair - - y tales of love. And gen - tle ga - zelles are
p
Ped.
roam - - - ing, And play the hap - py night long, While
Ped.
cre -

cre - - - - scen - - - - - - - - do
dim.
flows the might - y riv - - - er, With gol - den whis - per'd
scen - - - - - - - - do
dim.
p
cresc.
song, While flows the might - y riv - - - - - - -
pp
p
- - - er, With gol - den whis - per'd song.
p
cresc.
f
cresc.
And there 'neath the palm - trees shad - y
dim.
p

Where scent - ed winds breathe light, Our hearts shall sink to
cresc.
slum - ber, Shall dream of rap - ture to - night! Shall
cresc.
f
f
cresc.
dim.
dream of rap - ture to - night!
dim.
p
dim.
Dream to - night!
pp

BEETHOVEN'S FIFTH SYMPHONY.
FIRST MOVEMENT.

Arranged by LANDON RONALD
and ERNEST AUSTIN.

L. Van BEETHOVEN, Op. 67.

Horns
ff
sf
sf
sf
Strings
p dolce
Clarinet
Flute
Strings
p
Sub. p e crescendo
ff Full Orch.
ff
2

Clarinets
ff
Horns
Strings
ff
Violins
p
Clarinets
p
Violins
Clarinets
Violins
cresc.
subito
p
cresc.
subito
p
R.H.
L.H.
cresc.
f
piu f
ff

sf
sf
sf
sf
sf
sf
sf
Wood-wind
ff
sempre ff
Strings
Wood-wind
Strings
sf
sf
dim.
p
sempre piu p
pp
Ped.
Ped.
Ped.
Ped.
ff
sf
sf
sf
pp
Wood-wind
Strings
pp
Ped.
f
ff
senza rall.
ff poco rall.
Strings
p

Bassoons
cantabile
cresc.
Oboe
f adagio
Strings
p
a tempo
cresc.
Wood-wind and
Horns added
f
sf
f Full Orch.
Ped.
ff
1

Bassoons
Strings
f
sf
sf
sf
p dolce
Horns added
Wood-wind
Strings
Wood-wind
p
Strings
Bassoon
cresc.
Wood-wind added
sf Full Orch

Clarinets, Bassoons & Horns.
1
Full Orch.

LOWE & BRYDONE PRINTERS LTD. LONDON, N.W. 10.

The Second Movement of this Symphony will be issued in the next Part.

I FOUND A PARADISE.

Words by
EDWARD LOCKTON.

Music by
DOROTHY FORSTER.

"I found a Paradise" is published separately in the keys of E♭, and F. at 2/- net.
Obtainable of all music sellers.

The lone - ly hours grew glad, my tears were gone,
Be - cause a world of love at last was
mine!
mf
Be ev - er near my heart through all the years,
mp

O shine on me, dear eyes, like stars a - bove;
My prayer shall be that God may keep our world
An earth - ly par - a - dise, a heav'n of
love!
8va
p

DAPHNE.

Intermezzo de Salon.

THOMAS F. DUNHILL.

"Daphne" is published separately at 2/- net.
Obtainable of all music sellers.

mp
p
tr
f
mp

mf
ff

p subito.
cresc.
f
ff
dim molto.
p
leggiero.
pp

poco rit.
a tempo.
dolce.
tr
f
3

p delicato.
cresc.
f
f
ff
p
sff

THE ASRA.

Moderato.
Rubinstein, Op. 32. No. 6.
VOICE.
PIANO.
p
Through the gar - den still and lone - ly, Walked the daugh - ter
of the Sul - tan, In the sun - set by the foun - tain, Where the crys - tal
mf
wa-ters mur - mur'd. Stood the Slave with - in that gar - den In the sun - set
by the foun - tain, Where the crys - tal wa - - ters mur - - - -

dim.
mur'd; Dai - ly grew he pale and pa - ler, pale and
dim.
dim.
dim.
pa - ler, Till one ev' - ning came the Prin - cess, To the wait - ing
p
p
Slave she spoke then, "Tell to me thy name, I pray thee,
stringendo
stringendo
Tell me of thy home, thy kins - men!" And the Slave re - plied: "My
ritard.
ritard.

a tempo
name is Ma-ho-met, I come from Ye - men, And my
a tempo
f
f
race is that of As - ra, Who must sure-ly die, when their
love wakes, And my race is that of As - ra, Who must sure-ly die, when their
rall.
rall.
p
p
love wakes!"
p
rit.

MINUET.
FROM THE OPERA. "PAGLIACCI."

R. LEONCAVALLO.

"Minuet" from "Pagliacci" is published separately at 2/- net.
Obtainable of all music sellers.

sf
L.H.
R.H.
9
3
7
L.H.
R.H.
sf
9
L.H.
R.H.
3
8
L.H.
R.H.

sf
9
L. H.
R. H.
3
7
L. H.
R. H.
sf
9
L. H.
R. H.
3
8
L. H.
R. H.

BEETHOVEN'S FIFTH SYMPHONY.

SECOND MOVEMENT.

Arranged by LANDON RONALD
and ERNEST AUSTIN.

L. Van BEETHOVEN, Op. 67.

Strings & Bassoons
semprepp
cresc.
cantabile
f
f
p Violas and Cellos
dolce
f
p
cresc.
f
p
Wood-wind
cresc.
p
pStrings
Bassoons added
cresc.
f
Clarinets added
subito
p
Wood-wind
Strings added
f
p
pp
ff
Full Orch.
Ped.

Oboes &
Horns
ff
Trumpets added
Ped.
Ped.
Ped.
sf
f
Strings
pp
Cellos
pp
sempre pp
cresc.
f
ff
p
Violas & Cellos
dolce
e cantabile
pp
Violins
dolce

Violas & Cellos
sempre pp
f
Full Orch.
ff
short pause
pp
Strings
Clarinet
dolce
sempre p
Bassoon
Flute
dolce
Oboe

p Clarinets
p Strings
Wood-wind
f Horns
ff Full orch.
p
Strings
più p
pp
Cello
pp
pp

Wood-wind added
p mark the melody in the bass
cresc.
Flute
f
p dolce
Clarinet
p
Violins
Violas
cresc.
Cellos & Basses
pp
2nd Violins
1st Violins
Flute
ff Full orch.
sf

sf
p dolce
con molto espressione
p
Più mosso.
Bassoon
dolce
pp
Strings
mark the bass
Violins
cresc.
Cellos
f
Wood-wind added
p cresc.
f
p cresc.

The Third Movement of this Symphony will be issued in the next Part.

LOWE & BRYDONE LTD. MUSIC PRINTERS, LONDON, N. W. 10.

The Sundial in My Garden.

Words by
DOUGLAS FURBER.

Music by
A. EMMETT ADAMS.

"The Sundial in my Garden" is published separately in the keys of E♭. F. and G. at 2/- net.
Obtainable of all music sellers.

cresc e poco accel.
knows my ev - 'ry se - cret, and in its old-world way, My
cresc. colla voce.
mp a tempo.
rit.
love dreams for to - mor - row my thoughts of yes - ter - day.
mp a tempo
rit.
REFRAIN.
a tempo.
The old Sun - dial in my gar - den tells the sun - ny
mf a tempo.
hours; The hour for love, the hour for life, the time of sum - mer

flow'rs. And love dwells there with the ro - ses, As it used to
be My old Sun - dial in my gar - den Tells of your love for me.
mf
L.H.
In my gar - den of true
mp
calmo semplice.
lov - - ing it guards the flight of dreams, And

bids my love be hap - py from dawn till moon-light gleams. When
cresc
cresc e poco accel.
pp
ev - en - tide is call - ing and star-light dawns a - new, It
colla voce.
pp
a tempo.
brings life's great-est bless - ing, a dream of love and you.
L. H.
a tempo.
REFRAIN.
mf
The old sun - dial in my gar - den tells the sun - ny hours, The
mf
Ped.
*

hour for love, the hour for life, the time of sum-mer flow'rs And
love dwells there with the ro-ses, As it used to be My
old sun - dial in my gar-den Tells of your love for me. The
Tells of your love for me.
rit.
a tempo.
L.H.
1.
2.
f
molto rit.
ff
8

SUMMER EVENING

"Summer Evening" is published separately at 2/- net.
Obtainable of all music sellers.

cresc.
slent
mf poco più mosso
dim.
poco rit.
poco tranquillo
pp

mp
p
poco slent
mp
mf
dim.
p
pp
poco animando
mf
cresc.

poco piu moto
f
mf poco agitato
f
cresc.
ff (broadly)
dim.
poco slent
mf dim.
p
tenuto
p
più p

rit.
pp una corda
Tempo primo
mp
p
poco cresc.
tre corde
p
mp
p
cresc.
mf

f
mf
pp
mp
pp lontano
ten.
ppp
smorzando
col Ped.

FADELESS LOVE.

Johannes Brahms Op.3 No.1.

gath - er'd flow'r will sure - ly die, But a faith - - ful love must
stay!" "And thy vows, and thy vows, but heed - less words, To the
wind each dream now give!" "O mo - ther, tho' hea - ven and
earth pass a - way, In my bo - som this love must live! This
love, this love must live!"
agitato più f
più mosso
sempre rit. e dim. sin al Fine
pp

VALSE IN D♭.

OP. 64. Nº I.

CHOPIN.

Ped.
poco cresc.
dim.
p
cresc.
f

p
cresc.
cresc.
p
pp
poco cresc.
p
cresc. rit.
f

BEETHOVEN'S FIFTH SYMPHONY.

THIRD MOVEMENT.

Arranged by LANDON RONALD
and ERNEST AUSTIN.

L. Van BEETHOVEN, Op. 67.

poco rit.
Cellos & Basses
pp a tempo
Violas
Oboe
Horns
pp
Violins
cresc.
Full Orch.
f
ff
sf
sf
dim.
Cellos & Basses
pp

p Wood-wind.
Cellos.
f>p
f>p
Strings.
sempre p
Cellos & Bassoons.
cantabile
cresc. poco a poco al f
f
Full Orch.
ff
p

Very heavy
f Cellos & Basses.
f Violas & Bassoons.
Violins.
1
2
ff
f Cellos & Basses.
Violas & Bassoons.

Clarinets & Violas.
Violins.
Woodwind.
Flute.
Full Orch.
sf
ff
f Cellos & Basses.
dim.
p
Violas.
Clarinet added.
sempre più p
Violins.
pp

Flute.
sempre pp
Woodwind.
Cellos & Basses.
p
pp
Clarinets.
Bassoons & Horns
poco rit.
a tempo
p Bassoon & Cellos
p
Strings. (pizz)
poco ritard
Clarinet.
sempre pp
a tempo
delicato

Oboe
Strings &
Bassoon
Cellos &
Bassoon
pp
Strings &
Bassoons
Horns added
Oboe 8va
Horn
sempre pp
Strings &
Bassoon

⊕ This is the opening of the 4th movement, which will be published in its entirety in the next issue.

LOWE & BRYDONE LTD. PRINTERS LONDON, N.W. 10.

"I WILL NOT DOUBT."

*Words used by permission of Messrs Gay & Hancock Ltd.

10610-4

Tempo I°
"I trust in Thee!"
p solenne
I will not doubt, though all my pray'rs re-turn Un-answered from the still, white Realm a-bove;
I shall be-lieve it is an all-wise love Which has refused those things for which I yearn;
cresc.
dim.
And though at times I cannot keep from grieving, Yet the pure ar-dour of my fixed be-liev-ing, Un-
cresc.
molto rall.
Molto Adagio.
-dimmed shall burn Un-dimmed shall burn.
p Tempo I°
I will not doubt; well-
pp solenne

cresc.
an - chored in the faith, Like some staunch ship my soul braves ev - 'ry gale; So strong it's courage
mf
dim.
p
cresc.
that it will not fail To breast the mighty unknown sea of Death. Oh, may I cry, when
poco slentando a tempo
f
colla voce.
dim.
a tempo
rall.
ff Molto Adagio.
mf
mp a tempo
agitato
bo - dy parts with spi - rit, "I do not doubt," "I do not doubt!" Oh, may I cry, when
molto rall.
pp
bo - dy parts with spi - rit, Oh, may I cry, so list-'ning worlds may hear it, "I do not doubt!"
cresc.
ff largamente
"I do not doubt!" so list'ning worlds may hear it, With my last breath.
molto allargando
ten.
a tempo
If voice takes lower notes.
Ped.

CONSOLATION.

A. ARENSKY, Op. 36.

mf
f
f
crescendo
8
fff
8
p
mf
ritenuto.
mf
L.H.
p
a tempo
p
mf
mf
dim. e rit.
p
pp
molto rit.

ORPHEUS WITH HIS LUTE.

Words by
SHAKESPEARE.

Music by
ARTHUR S. SULLIVAN.

lute made trees, And the moun - tain tops that freeze, Bow them -
- selves when he did sing, Bow them - selves when he did
sing. To his mu - sic, plants and
flow'rs Ev - er sprung; as sun and show'rs There had made a last - ing
spring. To his mu - - sic, plants and flow'rs Ev - er sprung,
as sun and show - ers There had made a last - - - ing spring.
a tempo
cresc.
dim.
rall.
colla voce.

p cresc
Ev - - - - - 'ry
cresc
f
f
thing that heard him play, Ev'n the bil - lows of the
sea, Hung their heads and then lay
dim
dim
by, Hung their heads and then lay
p
p
tr
by.
f
dim
p
In sweet
p

mu - - sic is such art, Kill - - ing
rall.
a tempo
care and grief of heart, In sweet
rall.
p a tempo
cresc.
mu - - sic is such art, Kill - ing
cresc.
f
un poco più lento
care and grief of heart, Fall a - sleep, or
dim.
p colla voce
hear - ing die; Fall a - sleep, or hear - - -
pp
lunga pausa
- ing, or hear - ing die.
pp

CELEBRATED MINUET.

cresc.
f
mf

p dolce
mf
pp

BEETHOVEN'S FIFTH SYMPHONY.

FOURTH MOVEMENT.

Arranged by LANDON RONALD
and ERNEST AUSTIN.

L. Van BEETHOVEN, Op. 67.

Ped.
Ped.
Ped.
ff
f
Ped.
Ped.
p
cresc.
f
Ped.
p
f
p
f
pp
cresc.
Ped.

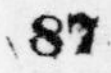

Ped.
ff
Clarinets Bassoons & Strings.
fp
p
Full Orch.
f
sf
più f
1.

2.
Ped.
Ped.
Ped.
Strings
p
Ped.
Horns &
Wood-wind added
Strings &
Wood-wind
p
cresc.
f
Ped.
Ped.
Ped.

Trombones added
ff
più f
crescendo
ff

sff
sff
sff
sempre ff
Tempo I.
Violins
dim.
pp
Strings
Clarinets
Oboe
Clarinets & Violas
Strings added

cresc.
Allegro.
ff
Full Orch.
Ped.
Strings Wood-wind added
sempre ff
Horns added

marcato
cresc.
pp

ff
Ped.
Wood-wind Horns & Strings
fp
p
f Full Orch
sff
ff
sf Strings

sf
sf
Wood-wind added
più f
Full Orch.
ff
ff
Bassoons
Horns
p dolce
Flute
p
cresc. poco a poco
Wood-wind added
Violas
Cellos
Basses
f
Full Orch.

p
f
Strings & Bassoons
p dolce
Horns, Oboes & Piccolo
p
Strings added
cresc. poco a poco
f
Full Orch.
Wood wind, Horns, & Strings
p
cresc.
poco
a
poco
sempre piu allegro
Presto.
fp
fp
fp
fp
cresc.

Lowe & Brydone Ltd. Printers London, N.W. 10.

THE TOP OF THE HILL.

Words by
LINDSAY CLIFFORD.

Music by
HAROLD SAMUEL.

10610-5

-dur-ance and pluck, Trust in him-self in-stead of trust-ing to luck, He must
toil might and main, or his toil is in vain, When once he's be-gun He must not
rest till he's won, But strive on and on with un-tir-ing will Till he's
climbed to the top of the hill. To the
p
cresc.
p
poco cresc.
poco dim.
senza rall.
p

REFRAIN.

top of the hill it's steep and it's long, For_ one road that's right you've scores that are wrong, And the
right road is lone_ ly,_ Seems to be on_ ly,_ Far-ther and far-ther a-
-way from you still: But_ don't stop and say the job can't be done, There's al-ways a way, the
goal can be won, Set doubt all a-side,_ With_a good swing-ing stride You'll
p
cresc.
mf
f

climb to the top of the hill.
Some-times you tire and feel you can't do your part, Ri-vals a-head may bring an
ache to your heart, You're tough and you're strong, yet the journ-ey seems long. When the
oth-er man's got all the best of the start; Speed up your pace and put your heart in your stride,

Now for the last few hun-dred yards that de-cide, Car-ry on, bat-tle on, its a
cresc.
fight for the right, Though- long be the climb, You're catch-ing up all the time, The
p
poco cresc.
rit.
a tempo.
top of the hill has-n't room for two, And the one that gets there must be you.
poco dim.
p-ff REFRAIN.
To the top of the hill it's steep and it's long For one road that's right you've
p-ff

scores that are wrong, And the right road is lone_ly, Seems to be on - ly Far_ther and far_ther a -
way from you still, But don't stop and say the job can't be done, There's al_ways a way, the
goal can be won, Set doubt all a_side, With a good swing_ing stride You'll climb to the top of the
hill. To the climb to the top of the hill.
p
cresc.
mf
f
1.
2.
rall.
ff

NOCTURNE IN F SHARP MAJOR.

CHOPIN Op. 15. Nº 2.

dolciss.
p
pp e poco riten.
cresc.
con forza
string.
m. s.
riten.
Doppio movimento.
sotto voce
cresc.
misurato
fz

cresc.
ff
decresc.
sf
più dimin.
pp
dimin.
molto rallentando
smorz.
Tempo I.
dolce
pp

leggierissimo
a piacere
con forza
fz
dim. e rall.
una corda
a tempo
pp
fz
sempre dimin.
poco rit.

THOU ART SO LIKE A FLOWER.

Words from HEINE.
Translation by ADRIAN ROSS.

R. SCHUMANN.

Slowly.

VOICE.

PIANO.

Thou art so like a flow - er, So fair and pure and dear; I look at thee, and sad - ness Fills all my heart with fear! I want to lay in bless - ing My hands up - on thy hair Praying that God yet will keep thee, So dear and pure and fair.

rit. rit - ard - an - do

Another setting, by Rubinstein, of the lyric by Heine will be published in Part 10. This will enable subscribers to compare the different musical styles of these two great composers.

ALBUMLEAF.

YORK BOWEN.

tempo
p
mp
espress.
cresc.
f
dim.
Ped.
ritard.
tempo
p dolce e espress.

poco accel
p
poco cresc.
dim.
rit.
tempo
p
mf
dim.
rit.
tranquillo.
p
pp
una corda
dolciss.
ritard
dim
Ped.

RHAPSODIE HONGROISE.

(HUNGARIAN RHAPSODY.)

No. 2.

F. LISZT.

capriccioso
dolcissimo
ten.
ten.
ten.
ten.
Ped.
tr
8
sempre pp leggierissimo
sempre giocando
p
più dim.
pp
cresc. molto

come primo
f
Ped.
rit.
riten.
a tempo
espressivo assai
sf
m.d.
m.s.
accelerando
crescendo molto
rinforzando
diminuendo molto
9
espressivo
p dolce
rfz
dim
piu p
dim.

dim.
rit.
un poco marcato rallentando
morendo
Lunga pausa
FRISKA.
Vivace
pp
pp
sempre pp
non tanto presto capricciosamente

poco - a - poco - accel - er - an -
- do - e - cres - cen - - do -
- - - - cres - cen - do - molto
Tempo guisto vivace
f marcato assai
piano scherzando
pp
pp
il basso sempre staccato
leggierissimo

Più mosso
pp
leggiero ma ben marcato
marcato
sempre piano, e poco a poco accelerando il tempo

stringendo
con strepito
a tempo
fff brioso assai
sf
con tutta forza e prestezza
di - - - - mi - - nu -
en - - - - do
p accelerando
Ped.

pp
Ped.
sotto p ma ben marcato
senza pedale
sopra
pp
p e sempre staccato
p e sempre staccato
cresc. molto
stringendo

rfz
a tempo
brioso assai
fff
sf
tutta forza
sempre ff
Ped.

8

poco a poco dim.

Ped. * Ped. * Ped. * Ped. *

8

Ped.

8

p un poco rallentando

*

Cadenza ad libitum

Prestissimo.

più riten

martellato

pp

cresc.

più cresc.

8

ff

Presto.

8

ff

Ped. *

Lowe & Brydone Ltd. Printers London, N.W. 10.